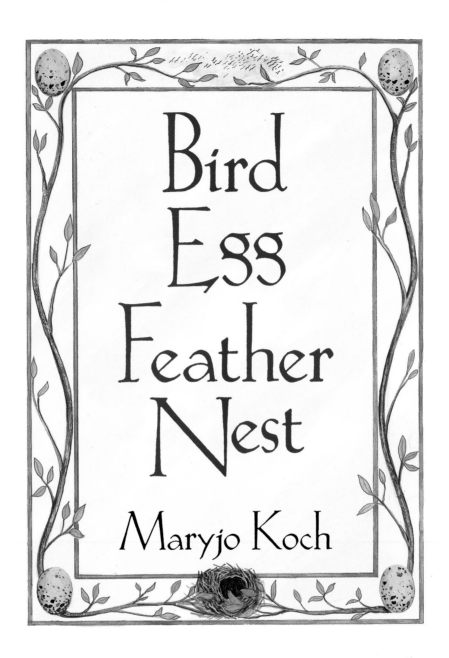

Bird Egg Feather Nest

Maryjo Koch

SWANS ISLAND BOOKS

SMITHMARK

THIS EDITION PUBLISHED IN 1998 BY SMITHMARK PUBLISHERS, A DIVISION OF U.S. MEDIA HOLDINGS, INC.,
115 WEST 18TH STREET, NEW YORK, NY 10011.

SMITHMARK BOOKS ARE AVAILABLE FOR BULK PURCHASE FOR SALES PROMOTION AND PREMIUM USE. FOR
DETAILS WRITE OR CALL THE MANAGER OF SPECIAL SALES, SMITHMARK PUBLISHERS, 115 WEST 18TH STREET,
NEW YORK, NY 10011; (212) 519-1300.

PUBLISHED IN 1994 BY COLLINS PUBLISHERS SAN FRANCISCO, 1160 BATTERY STREET, SAN FRANCISCO, CA 94111

A SWANS ISLAND BOOK

LIBRARY OF CONGRESS CATALOG CARD NUMBER: 98-60008

ISBN 0-7651-0762-7

PRINTED IN HONG KONG
10 9 8 7 6 5 4 3 2 1

In memory of Bob
and for our children
Wendy, Sunny and Jonathan

IRD

Evolutionary law determines what is essential.
No frivolous feature or unnecessary task is
perpetuated in a bird's life.

ARCHAEOPTERYX

CHRISTENED ARCHAEOPTERYX, MEANING "ANCIENT WING," THIS CREATURE POSSESSED AN AMAZING MIX OF REPTILIAN AND BIRDLIKE QUALITIES, AN EVOLUTIONARY MISSING LINK.

THIS FIRST BIRD, A MERE WIND-GLIDER, MADE THE INITIAL STEP TOWARD DEFYING GRAVITY. TODAY, THE MARVELOUS ABILITY TO FLY IS THE RESULT OF MILLIONS OF YEARS OF ADAPTATIONS:

AVIAN METABOLISM IS VERY HIGH IN ORDER TO PROVIDE ENERGY FOR FLYING. A HUMAN BEING WITH A METABOLIC RATE COMPARABLE TO THAT OF A HUMMINGBIRD'S WOULD BURST INTO FLAMES.

BONES ARE HOLLOW, LIGHTWEIGHT, YET STRONG. A PIGEON'S SKELETON, FOR EXAMPLE, WEIGHS JUST 1/20 OF ITS ENTIRE BODY WEIGHT.

AND MODERN BIRDS HAVE MUSCULATURE PRECISELY ENGINEERED TO MEET THE RIGOROUS DEMANDS OF SELF-POWERED, SUSTAINED FLIGHT.

The Feather Was The Dead Giveaway

THE CREATURE'S FOSSILIZED REMAINS, UNEARTHED IN 1861, INCLUDED THE DELICATE IMPRINT OF PERFECT FLIGHT FEATHERS, EXACTLY LIKE THOSE OF MODERN BIRDS. BUT THIS PIGEON-SIZE BIRD WAS MILLIONS AND MILLIONS OF YEARS OLD.

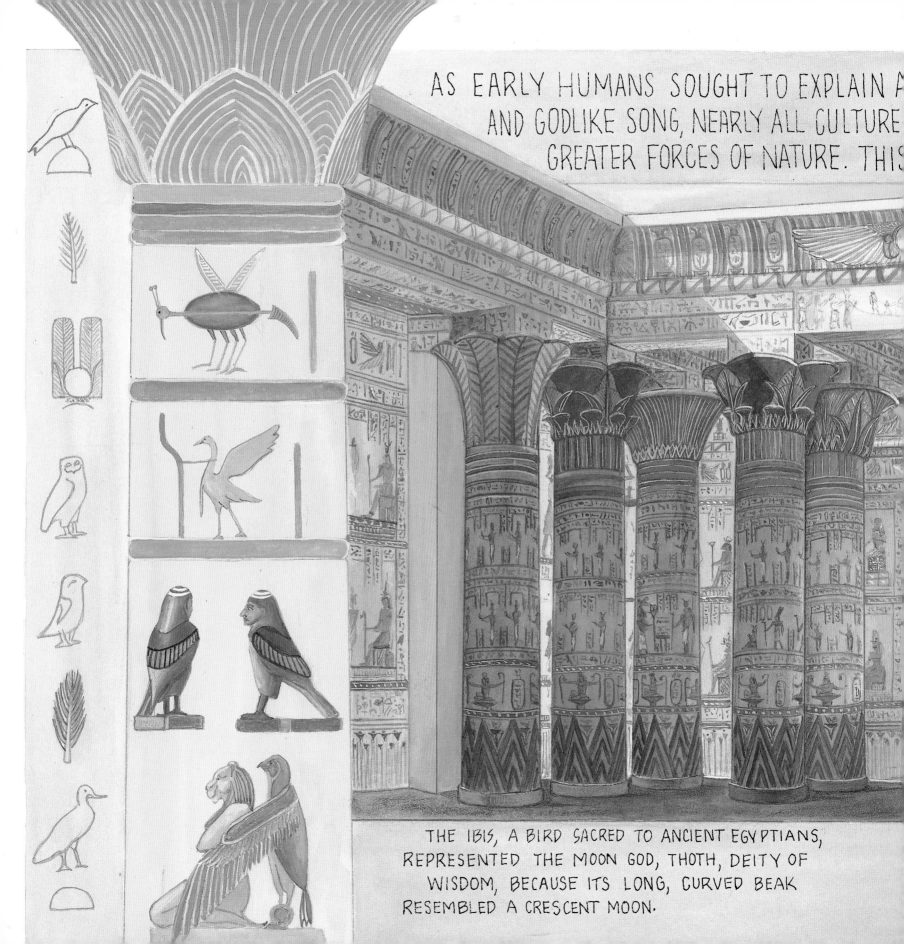

AS EARLY HUMANS SOUGHT TO EXPLAIN A
AND GODLIKE SONG, NEARLY ALL CULTURE
GREATER FORCES OF NATURE. THIS

THE IBIS, A BIRD SACRED TO ANCIENT EGYPTIANS,
REPRESENTED THE MOON GOD, THOTH, DEITY OF
WISDOM, BECAUSE ITS LONG, CURVED BEAK
RESEMBLED A CRESCENT MOON.

BIRD'S MAGICAL FLIGHT, UNEARTHLY BEAUTY,
CREATED FABULOUS MYTHS TO INTERPRET THE
WAS ESPECIALLY TRUE IN EGYPT.

IN ONE STORY, THOTH TOOK THE
FORM OF AN IBIS TO ESCAPE THE
FIRE-BREATHING MONSTER, TYPHON. THE
BIRD WAS OFTEN MUMMIFIED AND ENTOMBED WITH EGYPTIAN RULERS.

King Vulture

Greater Flamingo

THE AVIAN EYE IS A FOCAL POINT OF STUNNING BEAUTY AND COLOR, AND ITS SURERB CAPACITY IS EQUALLY REMARKABLE. IT PERFORMS ITS DUTIES SO SUCCESSFULLY THAT THREE OF THE BIRDS' OTHER SENSES -- TASTE, SMELL, AND TOUCH -- ARE LARGELY SUPERFLUOUS.

THE VISUAL ACUITY OF MOST SPECIES ALLOWS THEM TO FORAGE, AVOID PREDATORS, AND ADJUST FOR THE RAPID CHANGES OF AERIAL MOVEMENT, ALL AT ONCE. MEMBERS OF THE HAWK FAMILY HAVE EYESIGHT THAT IS ESTIMATED AT 4 TO 8 TIMES SHARPER THAN HUMANS', PERHAPS THE KEENEST SIGHT OF ALL LIVING CREATURES.

CLEARLY, A "BIRD'S-EYE VIEW" IS MORE THAN A MERE CHANGE IN PERSPECTIVE.

Wood Duck

Great Horned Owl

White Pelican

Toco Toucan

KIWI KIWI KIWI KIWI

FOOD FOR THOUGHT:

NEW ZEALAND'S KIWI TAKES 4 TO 5 DAYS TO DELIVER THE WORLD'S LARGEST EGG, RELATIVE TO BODY SIZE. IT CAN WEIGH AN AMAZING 25 PERCENT OF THE CHICK'S MOTHER, SOME 16 OUNCES OR MORE, AND IS COMPARABLE IN WEIGHT TO ANY NUMBER OF KITCHEN STAPLES:

4 STICKS OF BUTTER,

A BOX OF SUGAR,

A PINT OF CREAM,

OR, AS IN THIS CASE, ONE POUND OF UNCOOKED NOODLES.

ACTUAL SIZE

THE MALE ASSUMES COMPLETE RESPONSIBILITY FOR INCUBATION, WHICH CAN LAST NEARLY 2½ MONTHS. HE SOMETIMES EVEN SITS ON THE EGG FOR UP TO A WEEK WITHOUT LEAVING THE NESTING HOLE.

AT NIGHT THE BIRD BECOMES ACTIVE, WADDLING ABOUT THE UNDERBRUSH, SWEEPING ITS BILL BACK AND FORTH LIKE A BLOODHOUND AS IT SNIFFS OUT ITS EARTHWORM PREY.

THE TWO SHRILL AND MOURNFUL NOTES THAT FORM THIS BIRD'S CALL ALSO FORM ITS NAME: KI-WI.

CASP

TASMAN SEA

WEST CAPE

SOU

KIWI KIWI KIWI KIWI KIWI

KIWI KIWI KIWI KIWI KIWI
Stewart Island Kiwi
ONE THIRD ACTUAL SIZE
PACIFIC OCEAN
POVERTY BAY
HAWKES BAY
HAWKE BAY
MAHIA PEN.
NORTH ISLAND
C. FOULWIND
SEA
TASMAN BAY
LOWER HUTT
WELLINGTON
NELSON MARLBOROUGH
COOK STRAIT
ALPS
CANTERBURY
PEGASUS BAY
CHRISTCHURCH
CANTERBURY BIGHT
SOUTH PACIFIC OCEAN
SOUTH ISLAND
OTAGO
DUNEDIN
STEWART ISLAND
NEW ZEALAND
KIWI KIWI KIWI

THE KIWI IS NOCTURNAL AND SPENDS ITS DAYTIME RESTING IN ITS BURROWED NEST, OFTEN FOUND AMIDST A PROTECTIVE ENTANGLEMENT OF TREE ROOTS.

BRISTLY HAIR WHISKERS SURROUNDING ITS BEAK HELP IT DETECT MOVEMENT BENEATH THE LEAF-LITTER OF THE FOREST FLOOR.

A NATIVE OF NEW ZEALAND, THE EARTHBOUND KIWI LACKS MOST TRADITIONAL BIRD ATTRIBUTES: IT HAS EXCEEDINGLY POOR EYESIGHT, NO TAIL, AND ONLY THE HINT OF WINGS. ITS FEATHERS LOOK MORE LIKE AN OLD, SHAGGY COAT OF RUFFLED BROWN HAIR THAN INSTRUMENTS CONDUCIVE TO FLIGHT.

REGARDLESS, THE PEAR-SHAPED CREATURE IS WELL LOVED; LEGALLY PROTECTED SINCE 1908, IT SERVES AS THIS COUNTRY'S NATIONAL EMBLEM. PRIDE IN THE KIWI TAKES YET ANOTHER FORM:

NEW ZEALANDERS COMMONLY, AND AFFECTIONATELY, REFER TO THEMSELVES AS "KIWIS."

A HUMMINGBIRD MUST CONSUME ITS WEIGHT IN NECTAR DAILY, FEEDING EVERY 10 TO 15 MINUTES

... SINGLE DAY

... ITS METABOLISM FOR A SINGLE DAY

A MALE ANNA'S HUMMINGBIRD REQUIRES THE NECTAR FROM 1,000 FUCHSIA BLOSSOMS TO MAINTAIN ITS METABOLISM FOR A SINGLE DAY

HUMMINGBIRDS CAN BE FOUND ALMOST ANYWHERE FLOWERS BLOOM --- ESPECIALLY RED ONES.

Blue-throated Hummingbird Nest
ACTUAL SIZE

ED N. HARRISON
OOLOGICAL COLLECTION

Lampornis clemenciae bessóphilus

BLUE-THROATED HUMMING...

A.O.U. 427
SET MARK:
NO. OF EGGS: 0
SPECIES:
IDENTITY: Positive, confirmed by J. ...
SMALL EMBRYOS:
LOCALITY: MADERA CANYON, SANTA RITA MTS., SANTA CRUZ Co., ARIZON...
DATE: 20 July 1966
FRESH: SHOWING BLOOD:
INCUBATION:
DEPTH:
EGGS MEAS.: OUTSIDE DIAM;
NEST MEAS: INSIDE
NEST: Young bird observed on nest for three (3) days prior to ...
after nest had been abandoned for two weeks. Nest ...
of the Paper wasps suspended from an outside ...
summer home (southeast end of building) on Lot 55, Madera Ca...
COLLECTOR: Jack C. von Bloeker Jr.

ALTHOUGH IT SPENDS NEARLY ITS ENTIRE LIFE
AMONG FLOWERS, THE POOR HUMMINGBIRD
APPARENTLY CANNOT SMELL A SINGLE ONE.

FLYING FORWARD, BACKWARD, SIDE TO SIDE, UP AND DOWN, OR JUST HOVERING, THE WINGS OF A HUMMINGBIRD BEAT UP TO

FROM DAWN TO DUSK.

HUMMINGBIRDS DO NOT HUM --- THEIR VIBRATING WINGS DO.

TO ATTRACT A GARDEN OF HUMMERS, PLANT:
TRUMPET CREEPERS, NASTURTIUMS,
FUCHSIA, PETUNIAS, HOLLYHOCKS,
MORNING GLORIES, COLUMBINES,
DELPHINIUMS, SWEET PEAS,
CARDINAL FLOWERS, BEE BALMS,
CORALBELLS, SCARLET RUNNER BEANS,
SCARLET SAGES, GLADIOLUS,
SWEET WILLIAM, HONEYSUCKLE,
ZINNIA

DELICATE BUT LIGHTNING QUICK, THESE PENNYWEIGHT BIRDS ARE BELLIGERENT, TERRITORIAL, AND WILL TIRELESSLY DEFEND EVERY FOOD SOURCE IN SIGHT.

The Bee Hummingbird

IS A DIMINUTIVE RECORD-HOLDER:
AS THE SMALLEST BIRD IN THE WORLD
(NO LARGER THAN A BUMBLE BEE), A FEMALE
LAYS THE SMALLEST EGGS IN THE
SMALLEST NEST.

BEE HUMMER

HUMMINGBIRD

Anna's Hummingbird Nest
ACTUAL SIZE

SWORD-BILLED HUMMINGBIRD

Nesting Notes

TO BUILD
ITS THIMBLE-SIZED NEST, A
FEMALE HUMMINGBIRD SEARCHES
EXTENSIVELY FOR THE PROPER MIX OF
MOSS, LICHEN, LEAVES, FLOWER PETALS, AND
GRASS, AND BINDS THE POTPOURRI TOGETHER
WITH STICKY SPIDER SILK BEFORE LAYING
HER 2 EGGS.

75 TIMES A SECOND.

Shoebill Stork

LUNG FISH, GARS, FROGS, YOUNG TURTLES, CROCODILES

Sword-billed Hummingbird

NECTAR FROM TUBULAR FLOWERS

Great Hornbill

FRUITS, BERRIES, INSECTS, SMALL ANIMALS.

Shoveler

MARSH INSECTS AND VEGETATION

$\mathcal{S}$OME BIRD NAMES SAY IT ALL:
SHOEBILL STORK, SWORD-BILLED HUMMINGBIRD, GREAT HORNBILL,
SHOVELER, TAWNY FROGMOUTH, BOATBILL HERON.

$\mathcal{B}$EAKS HAVE EVOLVED INTO A GREAT VARIETY
OF SPECIALIZED SHAPES AND SIZES, WITH EACH INDIVIDUAL
DESIGN USUALLY ADAPTED TO A PARTICULAR DIET.

Tawny Frogmouth

BEETLES, CENTIPEDES, SCORPIONS, CATERPILLARS, MICE

Boatbill Heron

WORMS, CRUSTACEANS, FISH, AMPHIBIANS

The brown pelican population suffered serious collapse in the 1950s and 1960s due to environmental poisoning. Timely restrictions on the use of these toxins have encouraged the brown's steady comeback. Yet, it is no surprise that pelicans will not tolerate the presence of humans: they often regurgitate when man gets too close.

The highly social pelicans often fish communally, sometimes driving fish to shallower areas by whacking the water with their wings.

A brown pelican's dive is quite spectacular. From as high as 60 feet, the bird plummets and resurfaces moments later, with catch, it hopes, intact. Internal air chambers cushion the pelican's impact and help it to surface quickly.

A chick in search of food may nearly disappear into its parent's gaping pouch, filled with regurgitated fish.

Flying single file with synchronized wingbeats, then elegantly gliding in unison, they fly unlike any other bird. "Pelicans seem always to know exactly where they are going," John Steinbeck observed in THE LOG FROM THE SEA OF CORTEZ.

KING PELICAN BRAND
CALIFORNIA PEAS
PRODUCE OF U.S.A.
GROWN AND PACKED BY
F.S. AND F.E. KING
SACRAMENTO CALIFORNIA

Pelican

A MARVELOUSLY ENGINEERED CONTRAPTION, A PELICAN'S POUCH IS 6 INCHES DEEP WHEN EXPANDED AND HOLDS AS MUCH AS 2 GALLONS OF WATER. AFTER A SUCCESSFUL CATCH, A PELICAN CONTRACTS THE POUCH, SQUEEZES OUT THE WATER, AND SWALLOWS THE FISH WHOLE.

A PELICAN SOMETIMES DRINKS BY HOLDING ITS BEAK AJAR IN A DOWNPOUR.

ALCATRAZ, THE PORTUGUESE AND SPANISH WORD FOR PELICAN, IS DERIVED FROM THE ARABIC, AL-QADUS, WHICH MEANS TROUGH OR THE BUCKET OF A WATERWHEEL.

White Pelican
SOUTHEASTERN EUROPE, AFRICA AND ASIA
ACTUAL SIZE IS 65 INCHES.

Darzee the Tailorbird, immortalized in Rudyard Kipling's *The Jungle Book*, helped the mongoose Rikki-Tikki-Tavi fight "The Great War" against the big black cobra, Nag.

Long-Tailed Tailorbird Nest
ACTUAL SIZE
SIAM

"RIKKI-TIKKI-TAVI" 213

but he did not grow too proud, and
he kept that garden as a mongoose
should keep it, with tooth and jump
and spring and bite, till never a cobra
dared show its head inside the walls.

DARZEE'S CHAUNT
(SUNG IN HONOUR OF RIKKI-TIKKI-TAVI)

Singer and tailor am I—
Doubled the joys that I know—
Proud of my lilt through the sky,
Proud of the house that I sew—
Over and under, so weave I my music—
So weave I the house that I sew.

OVER."

A native of Southern Asia, the common tailorbird thrives in the most congested conditions right in the heart of bustling towns and cities.

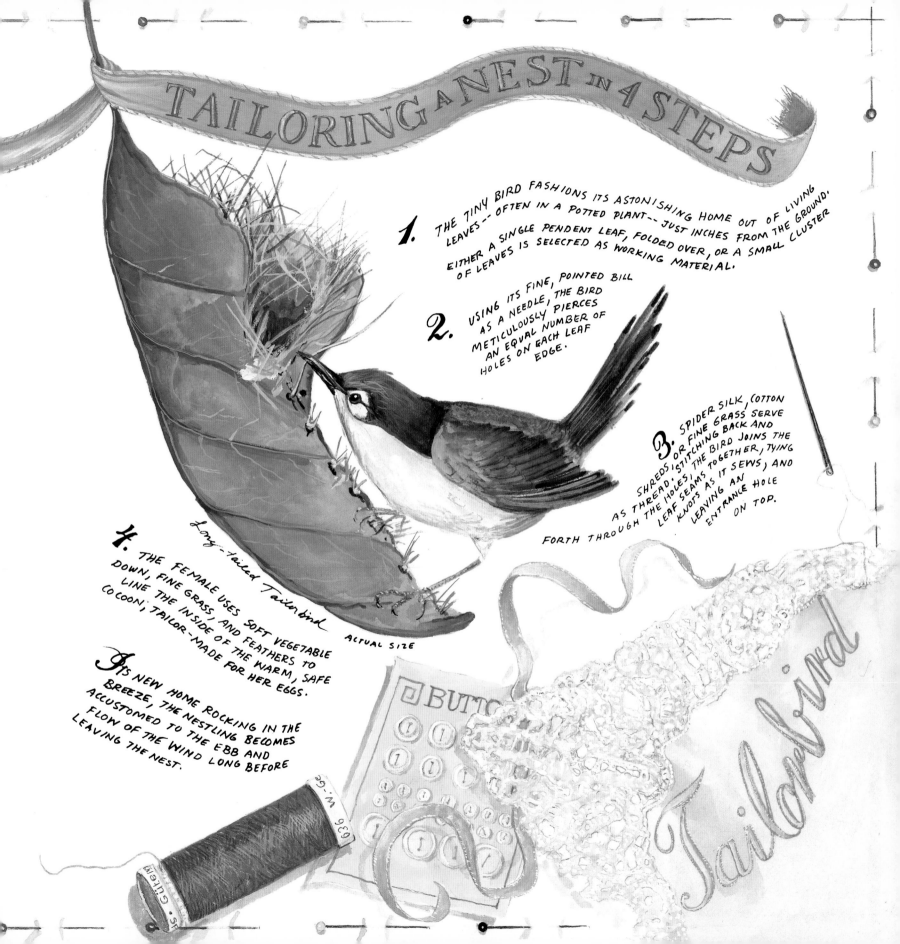

TAILORING A NEST IN 4 STEPS

1. THE TINY BIRD FASHIONS ITS ASTONISHING HOME OUT OF LIVING LEAVES—OFTEN IN A POTTED PLANT—JUST INCHES FROM THE GROUND. EITHER A SINGLE PENDENT LEAF, FOLDED OVER, OR A SMALL CLUSTER OF LEAVES IS SELECTED AS WORKING MATERIAL.

2. USING ITS FINE, POINTED BILL AS A NEEDLE, THE BIRD METICULOUSLY PIERCES AN EQUAL NUMBER OF HOLES ON EACH LEAF EDGE.

3. SPIDER SILK, COTTON OR FINE GRASS SERVE AS THREAD. STITCHING BACK AND FORTH THROUGH THE HOLES, THE BIRD JOINS THE LEAF SEAMS TOGETHER, TYING KNOTS AS IT SEWS, AND LEAVING AN ENTRANCE HOLE ON TOP.

4. THE FEMALE USES SOFT VEGETABLE DOWN, FINE GRASS, AND FEATHERS TO LINE THE INSIDE OF THE WARM, SAFE COCOON, TAILOR-MADE FOR HER EGGS.

ITS NEW HOME ROCKING IN THE BREEZE, THE NESTLING BECOMES ACCUSTOMED TO THE EBB AND FLOW OF THE WIND LONG BEFORE LEAVING THE NEST.

Long-tailed Tailorbird
ACTUAL SIZE

BUTTO

Tailorbird

S. Gütermann 639 W-639

In hunting its prey, a kingfisher brakes in midair before its plunge, or swoops down from a perch, seizing fish or land animals in its powerful bill.

Gray-hooded Kingfisher
AFRICA - ACTUAL SIZE IS 7 INCHES

Belted Kingfisher
ACTUAL SIZE IS 13 INCHES - NORTH AMERICA

Parent kingfishers teach their young to fish by dropping dead meals into the water for their retrieval.

Nesting Notes

Kingfishers are known for their burrowed-out homes which look like archaeological excavations in miniature. Built into the steep sides of riverbanks, a narrow tunnel -- from 3 to 6 feet long -- slopes up to the rounded inner chamber.

Shoveling with bills and claws, a foot or more is dug each day, completing a home in under 2 weeks.

Today, filmmakers find the kookaburra's distinctive call to be so euphemistically "tropical" that the sound is often edited into jungle scenes. This is a geographical impossibility, however, since this kingfisher is found solely in the savanna woodlands of Australia.

THE HYSTERICAL LAUGHTER OF THE KOOKABURRA -- A LOUD, UNSETTLING CACKLE HEARD IN THE EARLY MORNING -- ALARMED THE FIRST PIONEERS IN AUSTRALIA.

THE GIANT KINGFISHER OF AFRICA SOUNDS NOTHING LIKE ITS AUSSIE COUSIN. ITS LOUD AARK CRY, UTTERED IN FLIGHT, AND ITS CONSPICUOUS CHESTNUT BELLY-PLUMAGE, MAKE IT EASILY RECOGNIZABLE.

MOST KINGFISHERS ARE GREAT FISHERS, BUT THE KOOKABURRA IS A SNAKE-KILLER, TOO, OFTEN TARGETING A HIGHLY VENOMOUS CREATURE AND SHARING THE STILL-WRITHING MEAL WITH ITS YOUNG.

Laughing Kookaburra
AUSTRALIA - ACTUAL SIZE IS 17 INCHES

Kingfisher

Wood Duck

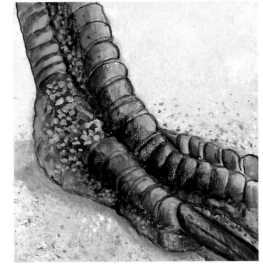

Double-wattled Cassowary

Blue Grosbeak

Red-headed Woodpecker

Coot

Dusky Horned Owl

African Jacana

Osprey

Common Fowl

WELL OVER HALF OF ALL 9,657 KNOWN BIRD SPECIES
HAVE THE ABILITY TO PERCH -- ON AN APPLE TREE
BRANCH, A POWER LINE, THE LIP OF A BIRDBATH, THE
BACK OF A LAWN CHAIR, A HUMAN FINGER, A LINE
OF CLOTHES HUNG OUT TO DRY . . . .

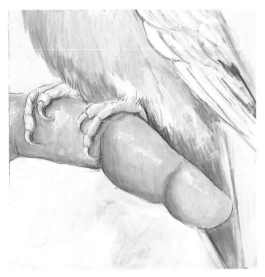

Parakeet

Ocellated Tapaculo

Hummingbird

Momentarily Earthbound

A TROUPE OF FLAMINGOS, IN POSITION, WAITING FOR.

A PELICAN LANDS, THEN WALKS RELUCTANTLY, AWKWARDLY, AS IF IT FINDS THIS HUMAN ACTION FAINTLY DISTASTEFUL.

THE TUXEDOED PENGUIN WADDLES ITS "CHARLIE CHAPLIN," SILENT AND COMICAL.

A HARRIED SANDPIPER SHOPS THE WATERLINE, THE INSISTENT WAVES ALLOWING NO TIME TO LINGER.

FADED SHRIMP TUTUS, POSE IN FIRST THE MUSIC TO RESUME.

A TIGHTROPE-WALKER, THE TOUCAN SOMETIMES LOSES ITS NERVE AND INCHES SIDEWAYS DOWN A NARROW BRANCH.

The ostrich's fluffy wings are no more than weak flaps with fans of 16 flight feathers each. Casting them like sails in the wind, the ostrich can run as fast as a gazelle -- up to 50 mph -- and can easily overtake many flying birds.

In males, the naked thighs and sparsely feathered neck are garishly colored, varying from flesh-pink in the Sahara to an astonishing bright blue in Somalia. These strong silent types belt out their hollow booming calls only in breeding season.

The lovable ostrich, 8 feet tall, bug-eyed, and with a neck as long and gangly as its legs, looks like a clumsy wallflower -- a frog in its throat and overdressed for the heat.

Ostrich

Succulent plants form the principal diet of the ostrich, but the birds are notorious scavengers and will readily swallow just about anything they find -- berries, seeds, small animals, even metal!

Flying is indeed for the birds, although only for lightweight ones. Physicists say that none heavier than 40 pounds can fly, which leaves the ostrich, the largest living bird, at a hefty 300 pounds, forever earthbound.

They are the only birds with just 2 toes, rather than 3, and are equipped with cushion soles that prevent them from sinking into loose sand.

Each female ostrich lays a clutch of about 10, but several birds often lay in the same place, creating an unmanageable pile of as many as 50 eggs.

Ostrich Feather - actual size

QUAIL, PHEASANT, AND PARTRIDGE HAVE CLAWS AS STRONG AND CLEVERLY DESIGNED AS A

A SINGLE MALE QUAIL WITH HIS FEATHERED HELMET, STANDS SENTRY, YEAR-ROUND, LIKE A QUEEN'S PALACE GUARD, PROTECTING BROODS OF UP TO 200 FEMALES.

King's Cadets
BRAND
CALIFORNIA GREEN
ASPARAGUS

LIKE A SHINING HOOD ORNAMENT AND JUST AS STREAMLINED, THE QUAIL'S BOBBING HEADPIECE IS MAINLY FOR SHOW..A TINY BOUQUET OF BLACK CONTOUR FEATHERS SLICKED UP INTO A FANCY COWLICK.

Quail Eggs

The California Quail

COVEYS HOLD A VIGIL AGAINST SURPRISE ATTACK BY PREDATORS. THEIR ALARM CALL IS PIT-PIT. IN EXTREME DANGER, SUCH AS WHEN UNDER ATTACK, THEIR CALL IS KURR. WHEN FORAGING AND MOVING ABOUT, THE COVEY CONTINUALLY UTTER THEIR UT-UT CALL TO MAINTAIN CONTACT. IF THEY BECOME SCATTERED, THEY SOUND THEIR LOUD CU-CU-COW CALL.

California Quail Nest   ONE HALF ACTUAL SIZE

THREE-PRONGED GARDEN RAKE. THEY EAT FOLIAGE AND WHATEVER THEY CAN DIG FROM THE GROUND, PRIZING PLANT BULBS, AND SEEDS.

A MOTHER PHEASANT'S CLUTCH ... UP TO 22 EGGS - HATCHES WITHIN A FEW HOURS. BUT BECAUSE HER GROUND NEST IS DANGEROUSLY EXPOSED TO PREDATORS SHE MUST LEAVE BEHIND THOSE YET UNBORN AS SHE QUICKLY LEADS HER RAMBUNCTIOUS NEW BROOD TO A SAFER SITE. THIS IS NOT AN ACT OF ABANDONMENT BUT SURVIVAL OF THE FITTEST; THE MOTHER BIRD INSTINCTIVELY KNOWS THE EGGS LEFT BEHIND CONTAIN DEAD HATCHLINGS.

It IS EARLY MORNING. SCURRYING ACROSS THE LAWN, A COVEY OF GAMBEL'S QUAIL WADDLE IN UNISON, IDENTICALLY DRESSED IN THEIR BEST GRAY FLANNEL, WITH PLUMED HATS WAVING, HURRYING FOR COVER.

poids net:

INGREDIENTS: SUCRE, GLUCOSE, PUREE DE MARRONS, NOIX, CACAO, OEUF ENTIER, MAT. GR. VEGETALE, AROMES NATUR

Chasse en Automne

Roger Guéres
CONFISEUR

COQ BLANC S.A. 93500 PANTIN

" ON THE FIRST DAY OF CHRISTMAS MY TRUE LOVE GAVE TO ME: A PARTRIDGE IN A PEAR TREE "

Quail Partridge and Pheasant

THEY'RE RELUCTANT FLYERS, ALL OF THEM -- PHEASANT, PARTRIDGE AND QUAIL. IN FACT, THE MONTEZUMA QUAIL IS CALLED "FOOL QUAIL" BECAUSE IT WOULD RATHER REMAIN STILL THAN MOVE AT ALL WHEN IT SENSES DANGER. A RELATIVE, THE MOUNTAIN QUAIL, MIGRATES 20 TO 40 MILES ROUND TRIP ON FOOT, NOT BY FLIGHT, BETWEEN BREEDING AND WINTERING RANGES.

Notes on Eagle Nesting

A BALD EAGLE'S NEST IS A MASSIVE HEAP OF BRANCHES, ROOTS, CORNSTALKS, AND RUBBISH THAT LOOKS LIKE A LARGE BONFIRE BEFORE A MATCH IS STRUCK.

THE NEST OF THE GOLDEN EAGLE, A GIANT, LOOSELY INTERLACED BASKET, HOLDS A COMMANDING POSITION ON A ROCKY CRAG OR CLIFF FACE. ONE SUCH NEST -- OCCUPIED CONTINUOUSLY FOR 35 YEARS -- GREW TO MEASURE 12 FEET DEEP, 8½ FEET ACROSS, AND WEIGHED AN ASTOUNDING 2,000 POUNDS.

SAW THIS GREAT PHOTO OF EAGLE'S NEST IN LIVING BIRD MAGAZINE

SPANNING UP TO 7½ FEET, A GOLDEN EAGLE'S BROAD WINGS PROVIDE MAXIMUM LIFT, ALLOWING THE MAJESTIC BIRD TO SOAR FOR LONG PERIODS WITHOUT LIFTING A FEATHER.

JUST FOOLS-IN-LOVE, A PAIR OF BALD EAGLES, IN A SHOWY COURTSHIP RITUAL, LOCK THEIR TALONS IN MID-AIR AND DESCEND IN A SERIES OF SOMERSAULTS BEFORE BREAKING APART.

Young Bald Eagle Talon

Golden Eagle Egg

EAGLE

THE DARK, PIERCING EYE AND FURROWED BROW FORM A MENACING PROFILE. ITS SHARP, CURVED BEAK IS DEFINITIVELY AQUILINE, A WORD STEMMING FROM THE LATIN AQUILA, WHICH, IN FACT, MEANS EAGLE.

AN EAGLE'S KILL IS QUICK AND CLEAN, A CLASSIC PORTRAYAL OF BEAUTY AND STRENGTH. THE BIRD DIVES TO THE GROUND, SINKING ITS FORMIDABLE CLAWS INTO ITS DARTING PREY, AND DEFTLY RISES BACK INTO THE AIR, TOWING A CATCH WHOSE WEIGHT MAY EVEN MATCH ITS OWN • THE BIRD'S SHARP TALONS AND BEAK ARE SUPERB INSTRUMENTS OF DEADLY EFFICIENCY.

Organized Labor
Proud and Free
USA 15c

THESE LARGE, POWERFUL PREDATORY BIRDS ARE A TIMELESS, WORLDWIDE SYMBOL OF STRENGTH, BRAVERY, AND SWIFTNESS.

Bald Eagle

THE BALD EAGLE'S NAME MOST LIKELY COMES FROM THE WELSH MEANING OF THE WORD BALD, WHICH TRANSLATES TO "MARKED WITH WHITE."

Bohemian Waxwing

Yellow-faced Grosquit

Bluebird

Black-naped Blue Monarch

Short-billed Marsh Wren

Saffron Finch

Orange-billed Nightingale-Thrush

Mistletoe Bird

Bush Warbler

To eat like a bird would be to choose from a menu including some none-too-appealing fare:

The Blue Bird INN
FOR THE BIRDS

Menu

Rain-washed *Lumbricus terrestris* 75
(COMMON EARTHWORM)

Poison oak berries 50

Hundred-legged centipedes 1.00

Carrion (PICKED-OVER, LEFTOVER) 90

Birdseed (THE EVER-POPULAR PACKAGED) 60

Crusts of bread (DAYS OLD)

BIRDS AND HUMANS HAVE SIMILAR NUTRITIONAL REQUIREMENTS-- PROTEINS, FATS, CARBOHYDRATES, VITAMINS, AND MINERALS-- YET DIFFER VASTLY IN WHAT EACH FINDS APPETIZING.

American Robin

Siskin

Tree Sparrow

Painted Redstart

Red-eyed Vireo

Ruby-crowned Kinglet

Painted Bunting

Yellow Wagtail

Golden-crested Mynah

Western Tanager

Blue Mockingbird

Love

The males of one species entice a mate by putting their best foot forward-- literally! The blue-footed booby, with very bright blue feet in sharp contrast with the dull brown plumage covering his body, performs an eccentric tap dance combined with elaborate high-stepping to catch his female's eye.

Initially, the male American redstart is extremely aggressive toward the approaching female. Quickly, though, the tables turn, and she becomes the antagonist, lunging at him and viciously attacking whenever he comes too close. Rebuffed, he becomes decidedly submissive, fluffing his feathers and humbly bowing to her.

As unromantic as this seems, these redstarts are engaging in a ritualistic courtship display which establishes the necessary rapport for mating. Romeo and Juliet they are not, but pair bonding appears likely for these "love birds."

Whether a single bird is seeking a monogamous, lifetime mate or a series of mutually satisfying nestings, most bird species participate each breeding season in courtship rituals, the prelude to copulation. Male birds generally attract and stimulate the females, although occasionally the reverse occurs.

The reproductive urge induces some truly peculiar behavior!

Love

Love

A ROWDY GROUP OF OVER 20 MALE RED-PLUMED BIRDS OF PARADISE CLUSTER IN A FAVORED TREE, RAPIDLY CALLING TO RILE THEMSELVES INTO A QUIVERING, ANTICIPATORY FRENZY. SUDDENLY WINGS ARE RAISED, TAILS ARE DEPRESSED, AND THEIR ELABORATE SIDE PLUMES ARE ERECTED IN A GLORIOUS, ARCHING CASCADE BEHIND EACH BIRD.

THE SHOW-OFFS, NOW MOTIONLESS EXCEPT FOR THE GENTLE RIPPLING OF THEIR DISPLAYED PLUMAGE, SUDDENLY BECOME WILD AGAIN, HOPPING MADLY ALONG THE BRANCHES AND CRYING HARSHLY.

THE MALE MAGNIFICENT FRIGATEBIRD OFFERS AN EQUALLY UNIQUE ENTICEMENT. HE INFLATES HIS THROAT POUCH (IT BULGES LIKE A DRIVER-SIDE AIR BAG) THAT SIGNALS LIKE A BRIGHT RED BALLOON TO FEMALES PASSING OVERHEAD.

Love

OTHER SPECIES HAVE MORE STRAIGHTFORWARD APPROACHES TO COURTSHIP. TERNS, KINGFISHERS, AND GREBES SHOW THEY ARE WORTHY MATES BY DISPLAYING FOOD OR NESTING MATERIALS AS A MEANS OF ESTABLISHING THE BOND BETWEEN MALE AND FEMALE.

THESE BREEDING RITUALS ARE NOT MERE FUN AND GAMES; THEY GUARANTEE THE SURVIVAL OF THE SPECIES. OVER TIME A COURTSHIP LANGUAGE HAS DEVELOPED TO ENSURE THAT EACH BIRD MATES WITH ONE OF ITS KIND.

$\mathcal{T}$HE MALE'S ELABORATE DISPLAYS OR BRILLIANT PLUMAGE ARE AN IMPORTANT PART OF THESE RITUALS AND CUE THE FEMALE TO SELECT THE CORRECT PARTNER EASILY AND QUICKLY.

$\mathcal{R}$EGARDLESS OF WHETHER DISPLAYS ARE SUBTLE OR FLAMBOYANT, THE RULE OF THUMB FOR COURTSHIP REMAINS BLISSFULLY SIMPLE: GET THE ATTENTION OF THE OPPOSITE SEX AND PROPOGATE. A BASHFUL BIRD WOULD HARDLY MAKE IT IN THE AVIAN WORLD.

Black Swan

Egg

PROPAGATION IS WORK. REAL WORK. HOW A BIRD MANAGES TO CHARM A MATE, DESIGN AND CONSTRUCT A NEST, INCUBATE EGGS, FEED HATCHLINGS INCESSANTLY, AND DEFEND ITS TERRITORY, SEEMS AN EXHAUSTIVE, IF NOT IMPOSSIBLE, FEAT.

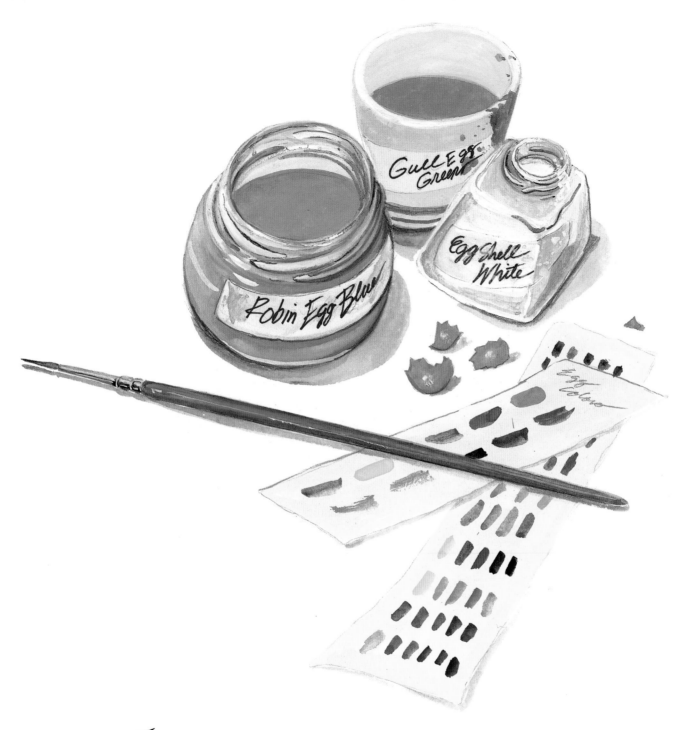

Egg colors

Robin Egg Blue

Gull Egg Green

Egg Shell White

𝓔GG COLORING IS A PHENOMENON THAT DEFIES SIMPLE EXPLANATION.

THE ACTUAL EGG PATTERNS, THE DISTINCTIVE BLOTCHES, STREAKS, SPOTS, AND SCRAWLS, ARE THE RESULT OF PIGMENTS ABSORBED BY THE POROUS "CANVAS" OF THE EGGSHELL DURING ITS PASSAGE THROUGH THE FEMALE'S OVIDUCT AND ARE AS INDIVIDUAL AS A HUMAN'S FINGERPRINT.

Camouflaging earth tones in ground-dwellers' eggs make sense, as do the bright whites of eggs from dark, concealed nesting sites, like holes in trees. But what of the glossy black of the emu and the electric blue of the heron?

Emu

Blue Heron

Actual Size

Actual Size

Evidence suggests that some species' eggs may not be highly palatable, and conspicuous coloring helps deter predators from such untasty targets. Other eggs may incorporate patterns that parent birds can easily recognize, as in the common guillemot, or may bear colors that effectively repel damaging rays of the sun, as in the American robin.

Thoughts on

cassowary   ACTUAL SIZE

Egg Laying

Once the female's ovum is fertilized, each chamber of her oviduct performs a specific function, turning the tiny structure into an exquisite egg. This process is so efficient and so perfected in some birds that they can lay an egg within 24 hours of copulation.

Once an egg is laid, it must be warmed for it to develop, a process called incubation. By choosing when to start incubating, each bird masterminds its own family planning.

Most ground-nesting birds rely on synchronous hatching as a means of survival so that their clutch can be moved all at once from the vulnerable nest site. To achieve this end, the parents wait until all eggs are in place before beginning incubation.

Other species stagger the arrival of young to avoid, in part, the instant, massive demands for food made by a nestful of newborns. These parents begin incubating with the first egg as soon as it is laid, giving it a head start over subsequent eggs.

THE SHAPES OF EGGS SHOWCASE NATURE'S TIME-PROVEN DESIGNS. EGGS THAT ARE LAID ON BARE, EXPOSED SITES GENERALLY ARE ROUNDED AT THE LARGER END AND ALMOST POINTED AT THE OTHER, THUS ALLOWING THEM TO ROLL IN CIRCLES RATHER THAN AWAY FROM THE NEST.

EGGS ARE ROTATED PERIODICALLY, PRESUMABLY TO HELP DISTRIBUTE HEAT MORE EFFICIENTLY, TO ALLOW EACH EGG A TURN IN THE CENTER OF THE NEST, AND TO KEEP THE EMBRYOS FROM STICKING TO THE INTERIOR OF THEIR SHELLS. THE AMERICAN REDSTART TURNS ITS EGGS ABOUT EVERY 8 MINUTES AND THE MALLARD DUCK PERFORMS THE ROTATION HOURLY.

ONCE THE YOUNG ARE BORN, THE EGG THAT SUSTAINED LIFE THROUGHOUT THE INCUBATION PERIOD SUDDENLY BECOMES USELESS AND DANGEROUS AND IS QUICKLY REMOVED FROM THE NEST. THE SHELL'S INNER WHITE LINING TOO EASILY ADVERTISES TO PASSING MARAUDERS THE NEST AND ITS PRECIOUS CONTENTS.

WHEN THE NUMBER OF EGGS BENEATH THE LAYING BIRD "FEELS RIGHT," THE PRODUCTION SYSTEM SHUTS DOWN. BECAUSE OF THIS INSTINCT, SOME BIRDS CAN BE TRICKED INTO CONTINUOUS LAYING. THE REMOVAL OF A LAID EGG PROMPTS THE LAYING OF ANOTHER TO FILL THE INSTINCTUAL QUOTA. A NORTHERN FLICKER PRODUCED 71 EGGS IN 73 DAYS IN ONE SUCH EXPERIMENT. IN OTHER SPECIES, THE PLACEMENT OF AN ARTIFICIAL EGG IN THE NEST ACTUALLY INDUCES PRODUCTION. FARMERS HAVE LONG PLACED "CHEATER" EGGS OF WAX, WOOD, OR PLASTIC UNDER HENS TO STIMULATE LAYING.

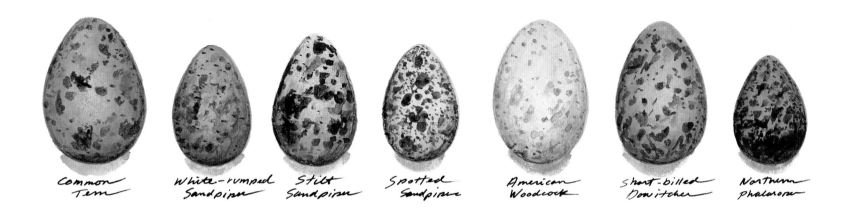

Common Tern   White-rumped Sandpiper   Stilt Sandpiper   Spotted Sandpiper   American Woodcock   Short-billed Dowitcher   Northern Phalarope

Nature carefully determines the optimum number of young that can be successfully raised by each species. Too few eggs and inevitable accidents threaten the entire clutch. Too many and the female may become too weak to survive the winter.

Killdeer   Dunlin   Wilson's Phalarope   Common Snipe   Rock Sandpiper   Pectoral Sandpiper   Arctic Tern

WHERE THE ENVIRONMENT WILL SUPPORT LARGER POPULATIONS, PARENT BIRDS "SENSE" IT, AND THE NUMBER OF EGGS LAYED (THE CLUTCH SIZE) IS ADJUSTED ACCORDINGLY. IN ONE EXAMPLE, THE AUSTRALIAN EAGLE INCREASED ITS NUMBERS FOLLOWING AN UPSURGE OF WILD RABBITS IN THE OUTBACK.

Cassins Kingbird

Zone-Tailed Hawk

Coot

White Ibis

Caspian Tern

Black Vulture

Noddy Tern

Ferruginous Hawk

Black Skimmer

Herring Gull

Eastern Kingbird

White-Winged Black Tern

Bridled Tern

Rosate Spoonbill

Least Sandpiper

Buff-breasted Sandpiper

Western Goshawk

California Gull

Ivory Gull

Scrub Jay

Greater Yellowlegs

Short-billed Gull

Little Brown Crane

Ruby-Throated Hummingbird

Red-Tailed Hawk

Great-Tailed Grackle

Black Oystercatcher

American Robin

Greater Black-Backed Gull

Grey Jay

Pine Grosbeak

Boat-Tailed Grackle

Ring-billed Gull

Aleutian Tern

Anna's Hummingbird

Brunnich Murre

Ostrich

Evening Grosbeak

Black Hawk

Long-tailed Jaeger

Black-necked Stilt

Black-bellied Plover

Wilson's Phalarope

Purple Sandpiper

Razorbill

Semipalmated Sandpiper

Yellow Rail

Stilt Sandpiper

Skua

Sage Thrasher

Broad-Winged Hawk

Rock Ptarmigan

Surf Bird

Painted Bunting

Black-Headed Grosbeak

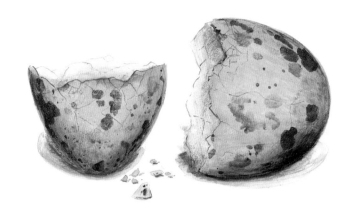

CRACKED, CRUSHED EGGS IN A NEST. SO MUCH UNHATCHED POTENTIAL.

THERE ARE TOO MANY EGGS WITH TRANSLUCENT, PAPER-THIN SHELLS TODAY, SMASHED LIKE MERINGUES-- NOT BY SURE-FOOTED PROWLERS, BUT, TRAGICALLY, BY THE FEATHER WEIGHT OF AN UNKNOWING MOTHER BIRD.

A BIRD'S EGG COMPRISES A WONDROUS BALANCE. IT BEARS THE WEIGHT OF AN INCUBATING PARENT, AND YET IS NOT SO THICK THAT THE GROWN HATCHLING CANNOT GET OUT.

BUT FOR ALL ITS MARVELS, THERE IS ONE FACTOR IN THIS DELICATE DESIGN THAT NATURE DID NOT CONSIDER : HUMAN BEINGS.

IN THE 1950s, HUMANS CREATED WHAT INITIALLY SEEMED A FARMER'S CURE-ALL : PESTICIDES.

POOF! WITH A DASH OF CHEMICALS, CROP-EATING INSECTS AND SMOTHERING WEEDS DISAPPEARED.

POOF! "UNAPPETIZING" SPOTS ON TODAY'S STRING BEANS, ORANGES, AND APPLES VANISH.

POOF, POOF!
SO DO BIRDS.

TOXIC CHEMICALS ARE NOT WELL TOLERATED BY NATURE; THEY MAY "CURE" ONE ILL, BUT THEY CREATE SO MANY OTHERS. IN BIRDS, THESE POISONS ARE INGESTED WITH THE FOOD THEY EAT, AND ARE MANIFESTED IN UNNATURALLY THIN EGGSHELLS.

CAMOUFLAGE

OVER TIME, BIRDS HAVE DEVELOPED THE REMARKABLE ABILITY TO MIMIC THE COLORS AND PATTERNS OF THEIR ENVIRONMENT. HOW FRAGILE AND VULNERABLE SOME BIRDS--AND ESPECIALLY THEIR EGGS--WOULD BE WITHOUT THE MAGNIFICENT DISGUISE OF CAMOUFLAGE.

HERMIT THRUSH EGGS ARE THE PALE BLUE-GREEN OF LICHEN AND OTHER MOSSES STREWN ON THE WOODLAND FLOOR. NIGHTHAWKS PRODUCE A SPECKLED PATTERN IMITATING THE GRIT AND GRAVEL OF THEIR SURROUNDINGS.

KILLDEER EGGS ARE MOTTLED WITH GRAYS AND BROWNS TO RESEMBLE THE STONES UPON WHICH THEY ARE LAID. BIRDERS RISK STEPPING ON THE NESTS THAT BLEND SO WELL INTO THE ROCKY TERRAIN.

THE EGGS OF A SHOREBIRD, WHICH HAS NO NEST, ARE LAID DIRECTLY ON THE BEACH. FOR UNWANTED PREDATORS, IT'S NEARLY IMPOSSIBLE TO FIND THEM HIDING INCOGNITO AMONG THE RANDOM SCHEME OF SHELLS, PEBBLES, AND DEBRIS.

The
Glorious Ostrich
lays the largest egg of any
bird alive. It is as big as a
grapefruit and as heavy as 4,500
hummingbird eggs or almost 3.3 pounds.
The smallest egg of the world's
tiniest bird, a hummingbird, is no
larger than a pea and barely
nudges the scale at
about .02 ounces.

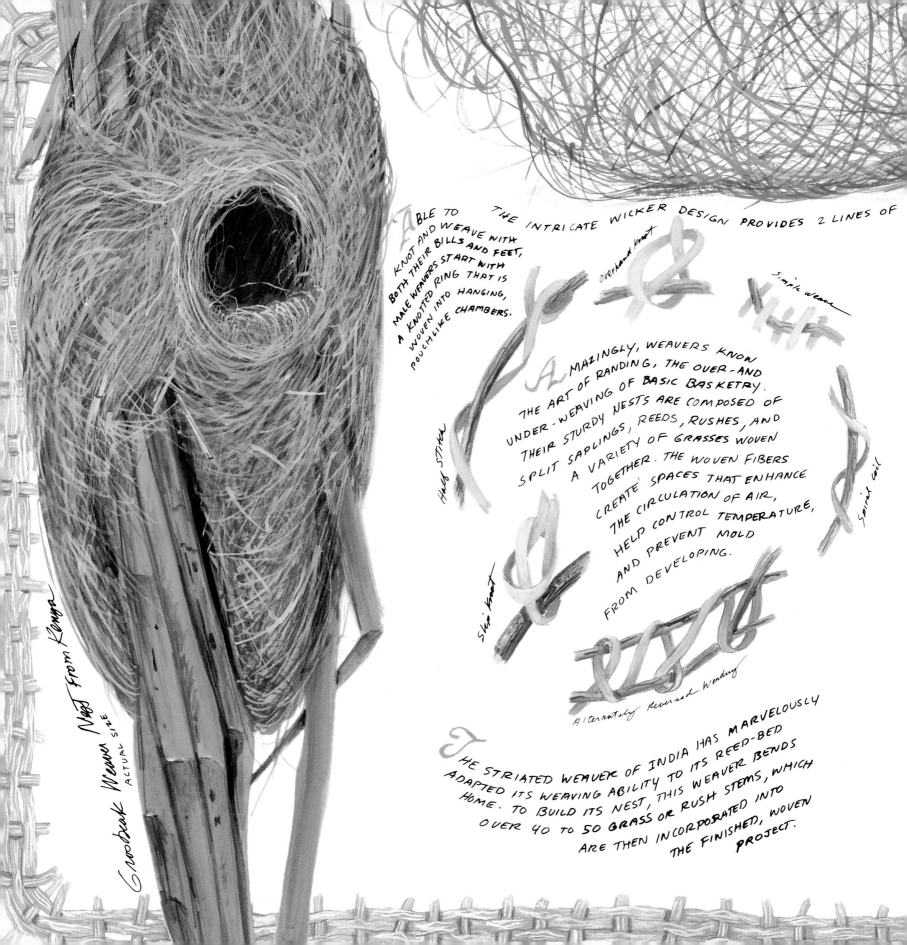

ABLE TO KNOT AND WEAVE WITH BOTH THEIR BILLS AND FEET, MALE WEAVERS START WITH A KNOTTED RING THAT IS WOVEN INTO HANGING, POUCHLIKE CHAMBERS.

THE INTRICATE WICKER DESIGN PROVIDES 2 LINES OF

Overhand Knot

Simple Weave

Half Hitch

AMAZINGLY, WEAVERS KNOW THE ART OF RANDING, THE OVER-AND UNDER-WEAVING OF BASIC BASKETRY. THEIR STURDY NESTS ARE COMPOSED OF SPLIT SAPLINGS, REEDS, RUSHES, AND A VARIETY OF GRASSES WOVEN TOGETHER. THE WOVEN FIBERS CREATE SPACES THAT ENHANCE THE CIRCULATION OF AIR, HELP CONTROL TEMPERATURE, AND PREVENT MOLD FROM DEVELOPING.

Spiral Coil

Slip Knot

Alternately Reversed Winding

THE STRIATED WEAVER OF INDIA HAS MARVELOUSLY ADAPTED ITS WEAVING ABILITY TO ITS REED-BED HOME. TO BUILD ITS NEST, THIS WEAVER BENDS OVER 40 TO 50 GRASS OR RUSH STEMS, WHICH ARE THEN INCORPORATED INTO THE FINISHED, WOVEN PROJECT.

Grosbeak Weaver Nest from Kenya
ACTUAL SIZE

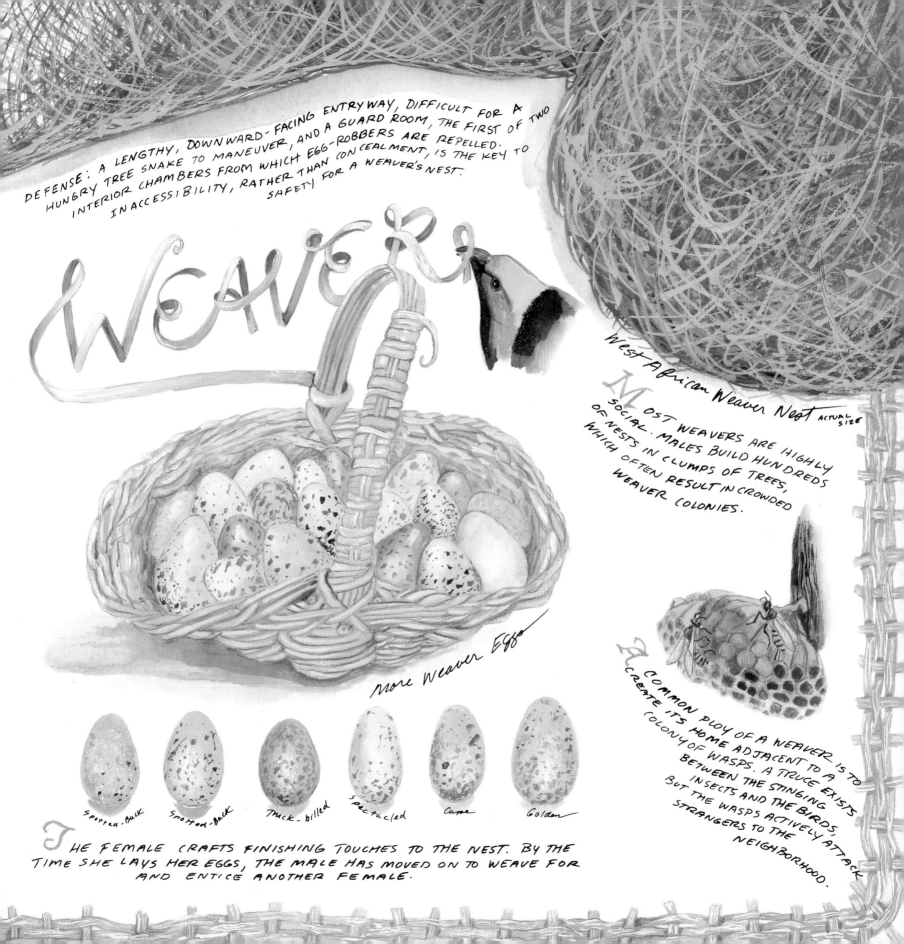

DEFENSE: A LENGTHY, DOWNWARD-FACING ENTRYWAY, DIFFICULT FOR A HUNGRY TREE SNAKE TO MANEUVER, AND A GUARD ROOM, THE FIRST OF TWO INTERIOR CHAMBERS FROM WHICH EGG-ROBBERS ARE REPELLED. INACCESSIBILITY, RATHER THAN CONCEALMENT, IS THE KEY TO SAFETY FOR A WEAVER'S NEST.

WEAVER

West African Weaver Nest ACTUAL SIZE

MOST WEAVERS ARE HIGHLY SOCIAL. MALES BUILD HUNDREDS OF NESTS IN CLUMPS OF TREES, WHICH OFTEN RESULT IN CROWDED WEAVER COLONIES.

More Weaver Eggs

Spotted-Back   Spotted-Back   Thick-billed   Spectacled   Cape   Golden

A COMMON PLOY OF A WEAVER IS TO CREATE ITS HOME ADJACENT TO A COLONY OF WASPS. A TRUCE EXISTS BETWEEN THE STINGING INSECTS AND THE BIRDS, BUT THE WASPS ACTIVELY ATTACK STRANGERS TO THE NEIGHBORHOOD.

THE FEMALE CRAFTS FINISHING TOUCHES TO THE NEST. BY THE TIME SHE LAYS HER EGGS, THE MALE HAS MOVED ON TO WEAVE FOR AND ENTICE ANOTHER FEMALE.

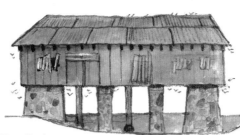

BARN SWALLOWS CHOOSE MAN-MADE STRUCTURES IN WHICH TO ATTACH THEIR HOMES, TO THE NEAR EXCLUSION OF NATURAL LOCATIONS.

CHIT-CHIT, CHIT-CHIT-CHIT, A BARN SWALLOW CALLS LOUDLY, SIGNALING DANGER WHEN INTRUDERS NEAR THE NEST.

CLIFF SWALLOW

BANK SWALLOW

TREE SWALLOW

BARN SWALLOW

VIOLET-GREEN SWALLOW

A PAIR OF BARN SWALLOWS ENGAGE IN A LONG, ARCING COURTSHIP FLIGHT, FOLLOWED BY INTERLOCKING BILLS AND MUTUAL PREENING.

Swallow

SPRITELY AND GRACEFUL, THE BARN SWALLOW IS AERODYNAMICALLY DESIGNED WITH LONG, NARROW WINGS AND FORKED TAIL.

MIGRATING SOUTH TO FLORIDA AND CENTRAL AMERICA, A LARGE GROUP OF SWALLOWS SUDDENLY DARKENS THE AUTUMN SKY. WHEN THEY DESCEND TO PERCH AND FEED, POWER LINES SAG UNDER THEIR WEIGHT AND FRUITING BUSHES ARE PICKED CLEAN OF BERRIES.

IF A BARN SWALLOW IS SIGHTED, ITS HOME CANNOT BE FAR OFF.

FAVORED NESTING SIGHTS ARE UNDER BRIDGES AND CULVERTS, BENEATH THE EAVES OF BUILDINGS, AND, NATURALLY, ON BARNS AND OTHER OUTBUILDINGS.

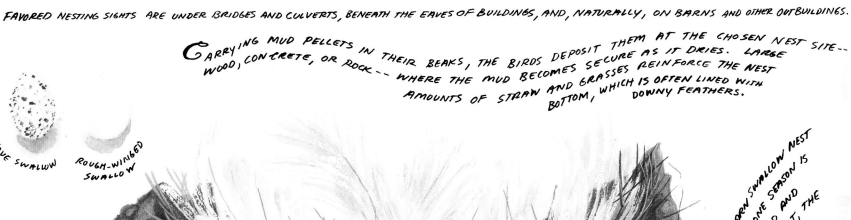

CARRYING MUD PELLETS IN THEIR BEAKS, THE BIRDS DEPOSIT THEM AT THE CHOSEN NEST SITE-- WOOD, CONCRETE, OR ROCK -- WHERE THE MUD BECOMES SECURE AS IT DRIES. LARGE AMOUNTS OF STRAW AND GRASSES REINFORCE THE NEST BOTTOM, WHICH IS OFTEN LINED WITH DOWNY FEATHERS.

CAVE SWALLOW

ROUGH-WINGED SWALLOW

A BARN SWALLOW NEST CREATED ONE SEASON IS OFTEN REPAIRED AND REUSED THE NEXT, THE YEARLY ADDITIONS GRADUALLY BUILDING IT UP TO A FOOT HIGH.

CLIFF SWALLOW COLONIES SOMETIMES INCLUDE CLUSTERS OF UP TO 3,000 GOURD-SHAPED MUD HOMES AFFIXED TO THE VERTICAL FACES OF CLIFFS AND CANYON WALLS.

BARN SWALLOW NEST   ACTUAL SIZE

Claude Monet

Jackson Pollock

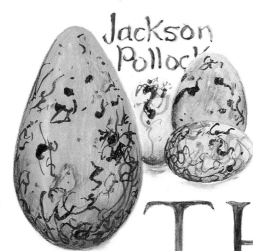

THE FINE ART EGG

Seurat

pastels à l'huile
"irisé"
oil pastels
boîte de 24 pastels assortis
pastels sets 24 assorted colors
SENNELIER PARIS

Vincent van Gogh

Camille Pissarro

Pelikan
DRAWING INK

MUSÉES N.
JEU DE
NATIONAUX
PAUME
DROIT D'ENTRÉE
13 F
297482
297483
DROIT
1

INSTITUT DE FRANCE
(ACADÉMIE DES BEAUX-ARTS)
MUSÉE MARMOTTAN
2, rue Louis-Boilly
Une Entrée: 15 F
Nº 645517

Turner

Pierre-Auguste
RENOIR

Édouard
Manet

SOVEREIGN 673 FRANCE

WINSOR & NEWTON
DESIGNERS'
GOUACHE
BURNT
SIENNA
DESIGNERS

LÉ 2210 ENGLAND

Masters
OF
19TH AND 20TH
CENTURY
ART
ADAPTED
A
WEALTH
OF
DECORATIVE
EFFECT
FROM
THE
EGGS
OF
BIRDS.

Feather

NOT ALL BIRDS FLY,
OR SING,
OR BUILD NESTS.
YET ALL BIRDS SHARE ONE FEATURE:
FEATHERS.
NO BIRD LACKS THEM OR CAN SURVIVE WITHOUT THEM.

*I*MPOSSIBLE AS IT MAY BE TO IMAGINE, THE FEATHER EVOLVED
OVER CENTURIES FROM THE FRAYED ENDS OF ANCIENT REPTILIAN SCALES.
GRADUALLY IT BECAME THE MOST COMPLEX OUTGROWTH OF SKIN FORMED BY
ANY ANIMAL, FACILITATING NOT ONLY FLIGHT, BUT INCUBATION,
WATERPROOFING, CAMOUFLAGE, AND COURTSHIP DISPLAYS.

Pheasant

A SINGLE FEATHER IS COMPOSED OF MORE THAN A MILLION
INTERLOCKING PARTS. BEAK TO TAIL,
MOST BIRDS ARE COMPLETELY
COVERED WITH THEM, WHETHER
WITH FLUFFY DOWN OR STREAMLINED
FLIGHT FEATHERS.

Downy Feather of a Peacock

Flight Feather of a Raptor

A RUBY-THROATED
HUMMINGBIRD IS DRESSED
IN LESS THAN 1,000
OF THEM, A TUNDRA SWAN
IN 25,000 OR MORE.

Hummingbird Feathers

Nature places stringent requirements on the mechanics of flight.

Too much weight, too little physical strength, too low a metabolism, and the bird never leaves the ground.

But the basic prerequisite of flight is the feathered wing. Light, strong, and flexible, the wing is an aerodynamic wonder, perfectly curved and streamlined to slice the wind while gaining its support.

PRIMARY FLIGHT FEATHERS

SECONDARY

FLIGHT FEATHERS

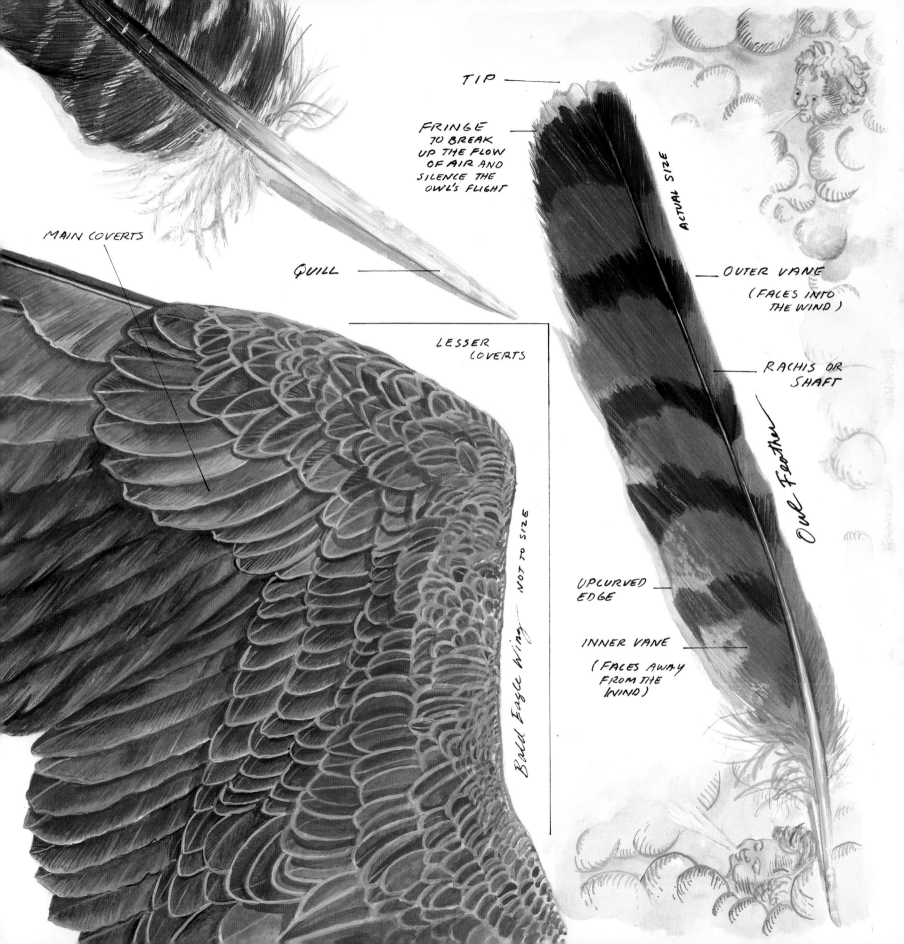

TIP

FRINGE
TO BREAK
UP THE FLOW
OF AIR AND
SILENCE THE
OWL'S FLIGHT

QUILL

ACTUAL SIZE

OUTER VANE
(FACES INTO
THE WIND)

RACHIS OR
SHAFT

Owl Feather

MAIN COVERTS

LESSER
COVERTS

Bald Eagle Wing — NOT TO SIZE

UPCURVED
EDGE

INNER VANE

(FACES AWAY
FROM THE
WIND)

THERE NEVER SEEM TO BE ENOUGH COLORS IN AN ARTIST'S PAINT BOX.

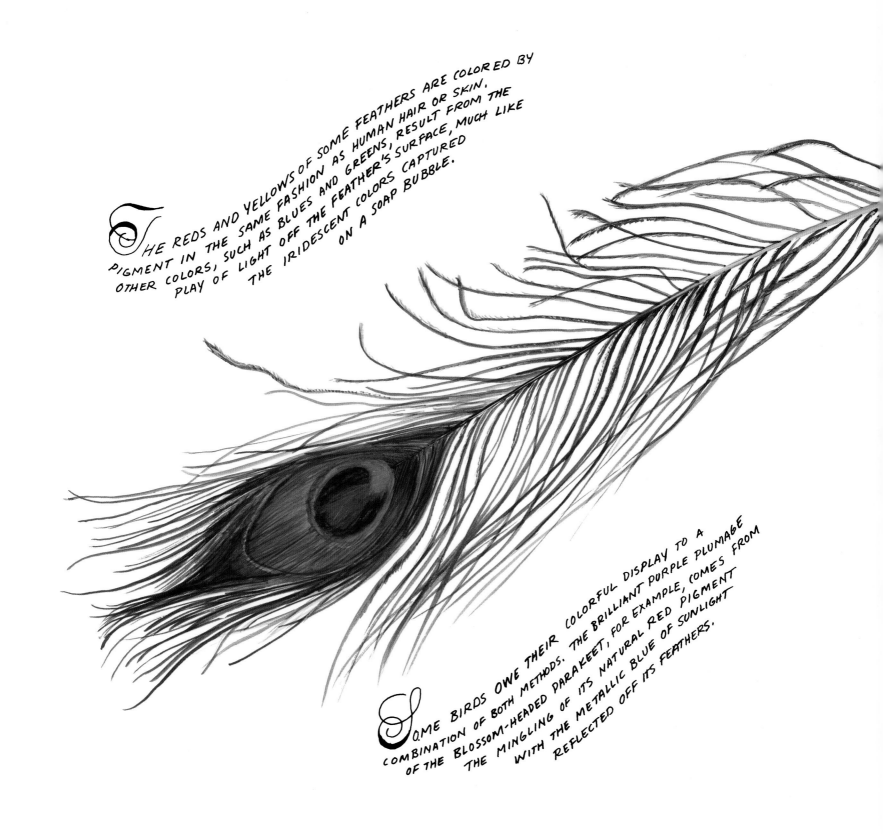

THE REDS AND YELLOWS OF SOME FEATHERS ARE COLORED BY PIGMENT IN THE SAME FASHION AS HUMAN HAIR OR SKIN. OTHER COLORS, SUCH AS BLUES AND GREENS, RESULT FROM THE PLAY OF LIGHT OFF THE FEATHER'S SURFACE, MUCH LIKE THE IRIDESCENT COLORS CAPTURED ON A SOAP BUBBLE.

SOME BIRDS OWE THEIR COLORFUL DISPLAY TO A COMBINATION OF BOTH METHODS. THE BRILLIANT PURPLE PLUMAGE OF THE BLOSSOM-HEADED PARAKEET, FOR EXAMPLE, COMES FROM THE MINGLING OF ITS NATURAL RED PIGMENT WITH THE METALLIC BLUE OF SUNLIGHT REFLECTED OFF ITS FEATHERS.

Pheasant

Woodpecker

Pheasant

Woodpecker

Macaw

Parakeet

Flamingo

Pheasant

Common Fowl

Dove

Pheasant

Pheasant

Common Fowl

Common Fowl

Owl

Parakeet

Parakeet

Pheasant

Pheasant

Wood Duck

Red Long

Parakeet

Grizzly Marabou

Guinea Fowl

Red Wing

Pheasant

Quail

Lovebird

Guinea Fowl

Goose

Grouse

Quail

Starling

common Fowl

Wood Duck

Scrub Jay

Woodpecker

Pheasant

Parakeet

Quail

common Fowl

Pheasant

Crimson Rosella

Peacock

Eagle Owl

Woodpecker

common Fowl

Woodpecker

MADE IN HAWAII *Aloha* MADE IN HAWAII *Al*

ʻIʻiwi
TWO THIRDS ACTUAL SIZE

Kapiʻolani Cape

Aloha

MADE IN HAWAII

COUNTLESS FEATHERS
WERE METICULOUSLY CRAFTED
INTO CEREMONIAL CAPES,
CLOAKS, LEIS, AND HELMETS
FOR HIGH-RANKING
NATIVE HAWAIIAN ISLANDERS.
INSTEAD OF JEWELS,
FEATHERS WERE USED TO
DENOTE STATUS, POWER,
AND REVERENCE FOR NATURE.
BEING WRAPPED IN A
GARMENT OF MAGNIFICENT
FEATHER WORK WAS THOUGHT
TO BRING ONE CLOSER TO THE
SUPERNATURAL WORKINGS
OF THE UNIVERSE.

TODAY MANY OF THE BIRDS
WHOSE COLORFUL FEATHERS
WERE USED IN THIS ANCIENT
CRAFT ARE EXTINCT, A SAD
LEGACY FOR AN ART FORM
MEANT TO WORSHIP NATURE,
NOT EXPLOIT IT.

Helmet of Ka-umu-aliʻi

Feather Lei

Aloha MADE IN HAWAII *Aloha* MADE IN HAWAII *Al*

FEATHERS ARE FROM THE 'Ō'Ō, MAMO AND 'Ō'Ū BIRDS

Akialoa ONE HALF ACTUAL SIZE

Mamo ONE HALF ACTUAL SIZE

Princess Ka'iulani wearing her feather lei

THE LEMON-LIME-COLORED 'AKIALOA, THE FIERY RED 'I'IWI, AND THE SUNSET-GOLD AND MIDNIGHT-BLACK MAMO ARE ENDANGERED OR GONE FOREVER, YET THEIR COLORS WILL REMAIN VIBRANT, IF ONLY AS FRAGILE MUSEUM TREASURES WHOSE INTERWOVEN MAGIC CAN ONLY BE IMAGINED.

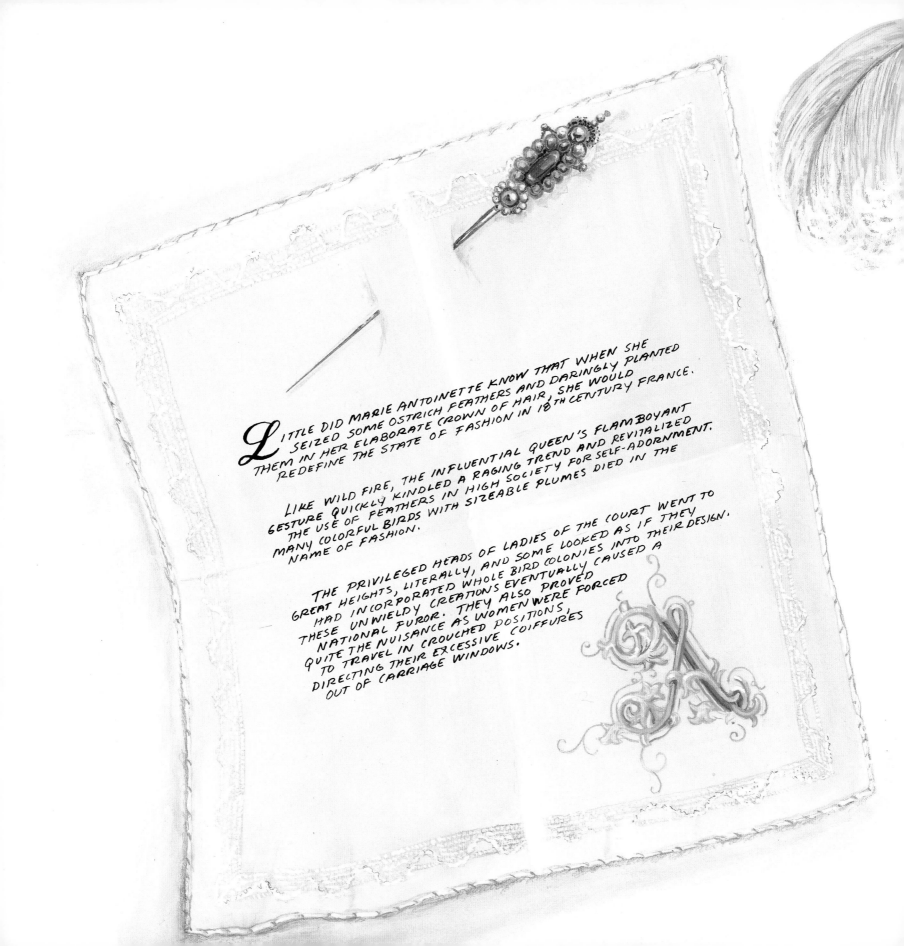

Little did Marie Antoinette know that when she seized some ostrich feathers and daringly planted them in her elaborate crown of hair, she would redefine the state of fashion in 18th century France.

Like wild fire, the influential queen's flamboyant gesture quickly kindled a raging trend and revitalized the use of feathers in high society for self-adornment. Many colorful birds with sizeable plumes died in the name of fashion.

The privileged heads of ladies of the court went to great heights, literally, and some looked as if they had incorporated whole bird colonies into their design. These unwieldy creations eventually caused a national furor. They also proved quite the nuisance as women were forced to travel in crouched positions, directing their excessive coiffures out of carriage windows.

SUNBIRDS ARE LAZIER THAN MOST BIRDS. ONCE IT CLAIMS A TERRITORY, A SUNBIRD WILL WAIT ON THE PERIMETER FOR HOURS UNTIL THE FLOWERS BECOME PLUMP WITH NECTAR.

BROWN-THROATED SUNBIRD NEST
EASTERN MALAYSIA - ACTUAL SIZE

SPIDER HUNTER
SUNBIRD
EAST INDIES
ACTUAL SIZE

COPPERY SUNBIRD NEST
SOUTH AFRICA - ACTUAL SIZE

SUNBIRD

BEAUTIFUL BUT LAZY, A SUNBIRD SPENDS NEARLY 65 PERCENT OF DAYLIGHT HOURS BASKING IN THE SUN. SHOULD IT BE VIEWED IN FLIGHT, THE SUNBIRD IS A FLASH OF RAINBOW, BRILLIANTLY COLORED IN METALLIC HUES.

RELATIVES OF THE HUMMINGBIRD, SUNBIRDS RESIDE IN A VARIETY OF HABITATS IN INDIA, SUB-SAHARAN AFRICA, MADAGASCAR, CHINA, NEW GUINEA, AND AUSTRALIA.

THEY ARE MASTERS OF ENERGY CONSERVATION: AT 11,000 FEET IN THE KENYA MOUNTAINS, THEY CAN LOWER THEIR BODY TEMPERATURE BY UP TO 17 DEGREES CELSIUS TO SAVE FUEL AT NIGHT.

A SUNBIRD NEST IS TYPICALLY A SUSPENDED POUCH WITH A SIDE ENTRANCE, AND MANY POSSESS ELABORATE PORCHES FOR PERCHING.

RED-CHESTED SUNBIRD NEST ACTUAL SIZE
UGANDA

Deep in the rain forests of Australia, it is business before pleasure for the eccentric male Satin Bowerbird. As part of his yearly breeding ritual, he constructs an elaborate platform of grass strands and erects twin walls (10 inches high!) at both ends of this stage. He then decorates this "Lover's Lane," or "Bower," with a mishmash of odd trinkets and scraps only he would consider treasures. His only criterion: that these items be blue.

Eminently pleased with his architectural prowess, the male Satin Bowerbird struts about his bower proffering bits of blue at the arrival of an appreciative female.

Satin Bowerbird
Australia — Actual size is 13 inches

Something old,
something new,
something borrowed,
something blue.

Satin Bowerbird's

Wish list:

- PIECES OF SHELL
- SNIPPET OF YARN
- BERRIES
- SWATCH OF FABRIC
- PEN CAP
- CLOTHESPIN
- SHARD OF GLASS
- PETAL PLUCKED FROM A FLOWER BED

But blue, only blue!

THE SATIN BOWERBIRD HAS RELATIVES WITH EQUAL FIXATIONS, SUCH AS THE MALE REGENT BOWERBIRD, WHICH HAS A PENCHANT FOR YELLOW AND SOMETIMES GREEN. COMPENSATING FOR WHAT THEY HAVE NOT INHERITED NATURALLY, LESS COLORFULLY PLUMED COUSINS ACTUALLY CONSTRUCT BOWERS WITH EVEN GREATER COMPLEXITY THAN THAT OF THE SATIN -- SOME WITH THE PRIVACY OF 4 WALLS.

LIKE FATHER, LIKE SON: YOUNG MALES VISIT THE SITES OF MATURE BIRDS, SHIFTING LEAVES AND TWIGS ABOUT IN THE ELDER'S ABSENCE, AS THEY MIMIC HIS BUILDING ACTIVITIES.

A TRUE LOTHARIO, A MALE BOWER MORE OR LESS IGNORES ANY FAMILIAL OBLIGATIONS: IN FAVOR OF MAINTAINING HIS BACHELOR PAD. THE FEMALE LEAVES HIS ABODE TO BUILD HER OWN NEST, SAUCERLIKE AND SNUGGLED AMIDST DENSE VINES UP TO 40 FEET ABOVE THE GROUND. SHE INCUBATES HER 2 EGGS ALONE, WHILE HER PROMISCUOUS MATE BREEDS CONTINUOUSLY.

Bowerbird

Bowerbird

Bowerbird

THE FINDING OF ONE RESEARCHER RAISES MORE QUESTIONS THAN IT ANSWERS: BUILDERS OF THE MOST ELABORATE BOWERS APPEAR TO LIVE THE LONGEST. WHY? ONLY NATURE SEEMS TO KNOW.

STREAK-BACKED ORIOLE

SPOT-BREA...

This "ENVIRONMENTALLY FRIENDLY" BIRD NOT ONLY RECYCLES PARTS FROM ITS PAST NESTS, BUT EATS INSECTS THAT WOULD OTHERWISE DESTROY TREES IN ITS NEIGHBORHOOD. LEAF-EATING HAIRY CATERPILLARS ARE A PARTICULAR FAVORITE.

Back AND FORTH, BACK AND FORTH, MALE ORIOLES COUNTER-SING A LYRICAL DUEL, IN WHICH ONE BIRD'S SONG IS PERFECTLY MIMICKED BY A NEIGHBOR. THIS HELPS REAFFIRM TERRITORY AND, INCIDENTALLY, MAKES FOR FASCINATING LISTENING.

Oriole

Baltimore Oriole

A BALTIMORE ORIOLE IS ESPECIALLY DEXTEROUS WITH ITS BILL, WHICH IT USES WITH GREAT SKILL TO WEAVE THE COARSE CLOTH OF ITS PURSELIKE NEST. ITS CONSTRUCTION IS SO STURDY THAT THE NEST OFTEN REMAINS ON THE TREE THROUGH THE HARSHEST OF WINTERS -- A BOON FOR BIRD LOVERS!

So MUCH ACTIVITY GOES ON BEHIND THE COVER OF LEAVES! ONLY AGAINST THE BACKDROP OF WINTER'S BARE BRANCHES CAN THE ORIOLE'S FINE WORKMANSHIP BE SEEN AND APPRECIATED.

AUDUBON'S ORIOLE

*L*ook for man-made materials in their hanging homes. Like many birds that live near people, orioles have an eye for items not normally found in nature: ribbon, string, yarn, and tissue.

HOODED ORIOLE

RD ORIOLE

*H*ung with care like a Christmas stocking, an oriole settles its home at the tip of delicate, flexible branches to deter unwanted visitors. "Rock-a-bye, baby, in the tree-top..." it sways like a rough-hewn cradle in the gentlest breeze.

Oriole Nest

THREE QUARTERS ACTUAL SIZE

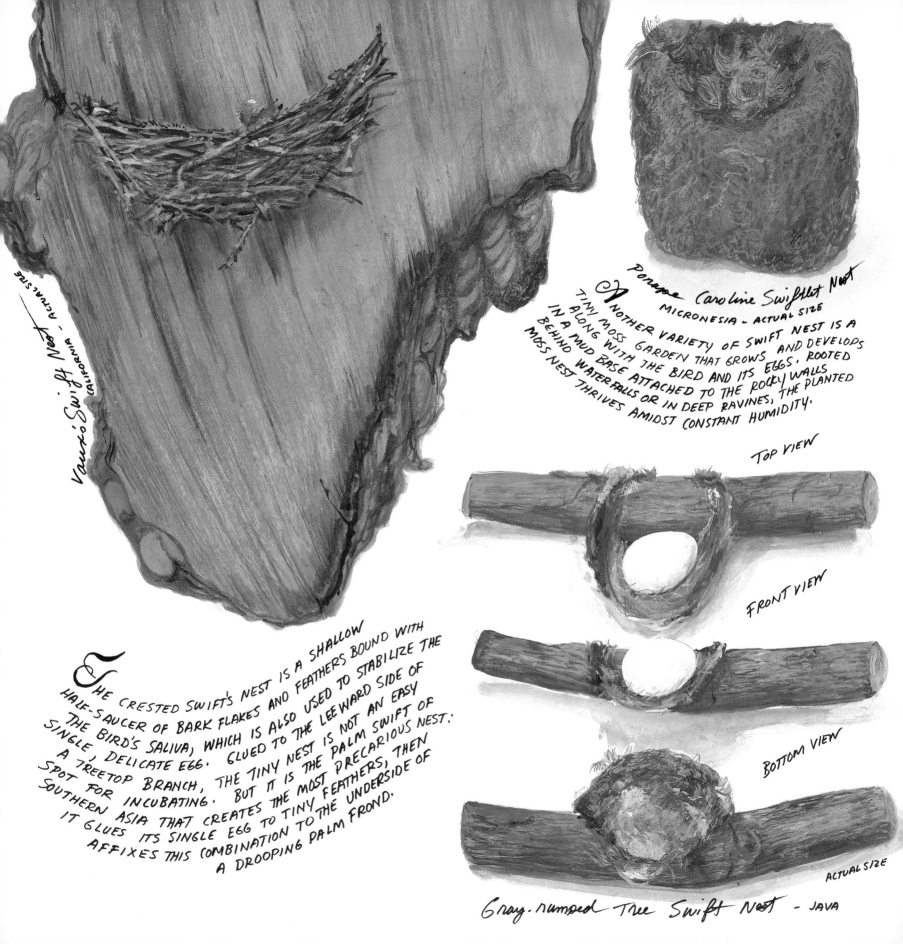

Vaux's Swift Nest - CALIFORNIA - ACTUAL SIZE

Ponape Caroline Swiftlet Nest
MICRONESIA - ACTUAL SIZE

Another variety of swift nest is a tiny moss garden that grows, and develops along with the bird and its eggs, and develops in a mud base attached to the rocky walls behind waterfalls or in deep ravines. The planted moss nest thrives amidst constant humidity.

TOP VIEW

FRONT VIEW

BOTTOM VIEW

ACTUAL SIZE

The crested swift's nest is a shallow half-saucer of bark flakes and feathers bound with the bird's saliva, which is also used to stabilize the single, delicate egg. Glued to the leeward side of a treetop branch, the tiny nest is not an easy spot for incubating. But it is the palm swift of southern asia that creates the most precarious nest: it glues its single egg to tiny feathers, then affixes this combination to the underside of a drooping palm frond.

Gray-rumped Tree Swift Nest - JAVA

When feeding its young, the European swift flies up to 500 miles a day in search of food. The parent returns to the nest hourly--far less often than other birds-- with up to 700 insects lodged in its gaping bill.

These birds have been clocked at 200 mph, though they more often fly continuously at an average speed of about 25 mph.

The European swift spends life on the wing. From dawn to dusk, it flies in pursuit of insects, dropping down to earth only occasionally to skim water from a stream or pool — never landing — then rising again in a graceful curve.

A swift has the remarkable ability to cling to sheer, vertical walls, but with its extremely small legs and feet, it cannot easily walk.

This stout-bodied bird can follow the erratic flight of insects with great speed and agility by alternating fast, air-slashing wingbeats with short glides.

One must voyage to southeast asia to find the gray-rumped swiftlet's edible nest, which is plastered high upon dark, cool grotto walls.

Bird's-nest-soup is apparently an acquired taste. It is served in the finest restaurants in china, yet the dish's detractors claim the delicacy is rather bland and could use a little tabasco.

Nests composed purely of a swiftlet's protein-rich saliva are called "white nests" and are most highly prized by bird's-nest-soup connoisseurs. "Black nests" are rejected because they contain straw, feathers, and bits of bark-- ingredients definitely not called for in any recipe.

There are approximately 20 species of "edible nest" swiftlets, tiny birds that sculpt hardened nests from their own sticky saliva, a painstaking process that takes over a month.

A.O.U. No.
WESTERN FOUNDATION
OF VERTEBRATE ZOOLOGY
Set No. 149,356
Edible nest—Swiftlet
Collocalia fuciphaga
Loc. Gomantong Caves Sabah E. Malaysia
Date 20 June 1963 Coll. C. Francis

Swift

Nest

"How hard to realize that every camp of men or beast has this glorious starry firmament for a roof! In such places standing alone on the mountaintop it is easy to realize that whatever special nests we make -- leaves and moss like the marmots and birds, or tents or piled stone -- we all dwell in a house of one room -- the world with the firmament for its roof,-- and are sailing the celestial spaces without leaving any track."

John Muir (1838-1914)

OF THE BRONZE-TAILED PLUMELETEER

COSTA RICA · ARCHITECT: BRONZE-TAILED PLUMELETEER · DATE: APRIL 8, 1988

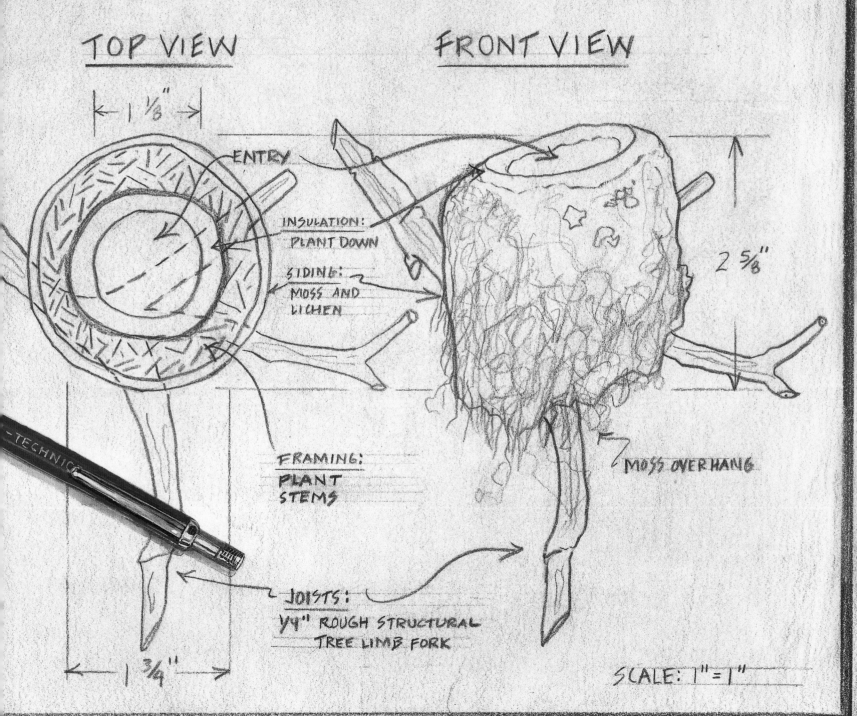

TOP VIEW

FRONT VIEW

1 1/8"

ENTRY

INSULATION:
PLANT DOWN

SIDING:
MOSS AND
LICHEN

2 5/8"

FRAMING:
PLANT
STEMS

MOSS OVERHANG

JOISTS:
1/4" ROUGH STRUCTURAL
TREE LIMB FORK

3/4"

SCALE: 1"=1"

FEATHERS   SNAKESKIN   HORSEHAIR   GRASS

STRING

STICKS

TIN FOIL

*N*ATURE ALSO PROVIDES THE NECESSARY TOOLS. WITH ONLY BEAK AND CLAWS (AND SOMETIMES THE HELP OF A PARTNER), THE BIRD CONSTRUCTS A SAFE AND STURDY CONTAINER FOR ITS EGGS, OFTEN USING THE CURVE OF ITS BODY TO MOLD THE PERFECT SHAPE.

*S*OME THINK THIS INSTINCTUAL ACTIVITY BEGAN WHEN A LACK OF NATURAL CAVITIES FORCED THE FIRST NEST-BUILDERS TO CRAFT SHELTERS THAT COULD BRAVE THE ELEMENTS AND PROTECT THEMSELVES AND THEIR YOUNG.

*T*ODAY'S BIRD SCAVENGES IMAGINATIVELY, PLUCKING RAW MATERIALS NOT ONLY FROM THE ENVIRONMENT BUT FROM THE LITTER OF CIVILIZATION AND THE FRUITS OF ITS OWN BODY AS WELL: COCOON SILK, SPIDER WEBS, AND ABANDONED SNAKESKINS; MUD, LEAVES, MOSS AND TWIGS; CELLOPHANE, NEWSPAPER, AND GUM WRAPPERS; SALIVA, PELLETS, AND FEATHERS.

*D*ESPITE OVERALL SIMILARITIES, EACH NEST IDENTIFIES ITS MAKER AS SURELY AS AN ARTIST'S SIGNATURE.

PINENEEDLES   TWIGS   SHOELACES

LEAVES   DRAGONFLY WINGS   PAPER   LICHEN

FINE GRASS
LINED CUP

THICK GRASS LINED
RIM AND
BODY OF
NEST

RIBBON

OUTER TWIG
LAYER

MOSS

SEED HEAD

MUD PASTE
LINING

Cut-away View of Robin's Nest
- ACTUAL SIZE -

BUTTERFLY WINGS   FLOWER PETALS   ROOTLETS   WOOL

A home is what one makes of it.

WESTERN FOUNDATION
OF VERTEBRATE ZOOLOGY
A.O.U.No. 719 K   Set No. 73,297
     Bewicks Wren   (719K)
     Thryomanes bewickii correctos
Loc. nr. SanAntonio Canon, LA.Co, Calif.
Date. 26 Apr. 1918   Coll by. W.M. Pierce

719 d
634
6

Mossy Birdhouse
-ACTUAL SIZE-

$\mathscr{B}$IRD-WATCHING RANKS AS NORTH AMERICA'S SECOND MOST POPULAR PASSIVE SPORT (AFTER GARDENING), WHICH MAY EXPLAIN THE PREVALENCE OF BIRDHOUSES THROUGHOUT THE UNITED STATES. IF IT IS NOT POSSIBLE TO VENTURE OUT INTO THE WILDS TO OBSERVE BIRDS IN THEIR NATURAL HABITAT, WHY NOT SIMPLY BUILD BIRD-SIZE HOUSES TO BRING THEM INTO ONE'S OWN BACKYARD?

$\mathscr{W}$HILE MOST BIRDS PREFER TO BUILD THEIR OWN DWELLINGS, NEARLY 86 NORTH AMERICAN SPECIES HAVE BEEN KNOWN TO OCCUPY ARTIFICIAL HOMES. HOWEVER, LIKE HUMANS, BIRDS PLACE STRINGENT REQUIREMENTS ON POTENTIAL HOMESITES AND WILL QUICKLY VACATE A BIRDHOUSE THAT IS NOT "UP TO STANDARD."

$\mathscr{S}$OME BIRDHOUSE BUILDERS SIMPLY HANG OUT THEIR CREATIONS AND SEE WHAT BIRDS (IF ANY) WILL MOVE IN, WHILE OTHER DESIGNERS RESEARCH THE REQUIREMENTS OF NEIGHBORHOOD BIRDS AND BUILD ACCORDINGLY.

$\mathscr{A}$NNUAL CONTESTS AND EXHIBITIONS TAKE PLACE AROUND THE WORLD IN WHICH PRACTICAL AND PURELY DECORATIVE DESIGNS VIE FOR TOP HONORS.

$\mathscr{U}$LTIMATELY, HOWEVER, THE TRUE TEST OF A "WINNING" DESIGN IS WHETHER OR NOT A BIRD WILL ACTUALLY LIVE IN IT.

ROBINS CAN'T REALLY HEAR THE LANGUAGE OF WORMS! STALKING ITS FAVORITE FOOD, THE ROBIN ONLY APPEARS TO LISTEN FOR THE SOUND OF THE WORM'S SUBTERRANEAN SLITHER AND SHIMMY. IN ACTUALITY, IT IS BY SIGHT THAT IT NOTES THE SUBTLE DISTURBANCES MARKING THE EARTHWORM'S ESCAPE. RUNNING, THE BIRD STOPS, COCKS ITS HEAD TO THE SIDE, THEN UNEARTHS THE DEFENSELESS MORSEL, EATING UP TO 14 FEET OF WORM ON A GOOD DAY.

ROBIN

IN ACTUALITY, A ROBIN IS A THRUSH. EARLY AMERICAN COLONISTS GAVE RECOGNITION TO A BIRD LOOSELY RESEMBLING A BREED FROM THE OLD WORLD. IT CAME TO BE KNOWN AS THE AMERICAN ROBIN, A DISTANT RELATIVE OF THE EUROPEAN ROBIN.

A MALE ROBIN IS SO MADLY TERRITORIAL DURING BREEDING SEASON THAT HE OFTEN BECOMES HIS OWN WORST ENEMY. SHOULD HE SPOT HIMSELF IN A PICTURE WINDOW OR A POLISHED CAR HUBCAP, THE UNWITTING ROBIN WILL ENGAGE IN A FIERCE BUT FRUITLESS BATTLE WITH HIS REFLECTION.

Voice
LOUD, RICH CAROLING WITH SHORT PHRASES THAT CHANGE PITCH: CHEERILY-CHEERY-CHEERILY-CHEERY; CALL NOTES: TUT-TUT-TUT OR ALSO SLURRED; TYEEP; IN FLIGHT: SEE-LIP.

ANYONE UNFAMILIAR WITH THE BLUE OF A ROBIN'S EGG MUST NOT HAVE CLIMBED ENOUGH TREES AS A CHILD.

A SANDPIPER'S NONSTOP SCAMPERING ALONG THE SHORE MAY CREATE A UNIQUE FORM OF CAMOUFLAGE. WERE THE BIRD TO STAND STOCK-STILL, IT WOULD EASILY BE SIGHTED AGAINST THE CONSTANT MOTION OF THE OCEAN BACKDROP.

American Oystercatcher
ACTUAL SIZE IS 1.8 INCHES

ACTUAL SIZE

OYSTERCATCHERS ARE FOUND (AND HEARD!) ON THE SHORES OF EVERY CONTINENT EXCEPT ANTARCTICA: NOISY BIRDS, THEY STRUT AND FUSS DURING BREEDING SEASON TO DRIVE AWAY INTRUDERS.

"CATCHING" AN OYSTER IS THE EASY PART; WRENCHING IT OPEN TAKES TALENT, AND THE OYSTERCATCHER IS PERFECTLY EQUIPPED FOR THE JOB. SNATCHING AN IMMOBILE OYSTER FROM ITS BED, THE BIRD PLIES THE 2 SHELL HALVES APART WITH ITS BLADELIKE BILL, AND CHISELS OUT THE MEAT.

Least Sandpiper
ACTUAL SIZE IS 6 INCHES

SANDPIPER BEAKS RANGE FROM THE VERY SHORT TO PINOCCHIO LENGTH, JUTTING OUT 8 INCHES. SIZE AND SHAPE DEPEND ON HOW DEEP INTO THE MUD, SAND, OR SILT THE BIRD MUST PROBE TO FIND ITS FOOD.

JUICE

Gulls tolerate humans and thrive among them. They also seem to share some distinctly human characteristics: their cries sound eerily like wailing voices; they live and loiter like beach bums on crowded stretches of sand; and these omnivorous birds will eat practically anything, from fresh seafood to discarded potato chips.

The tiny red dot on a gull's yellow beak is an easy target for nestlings: when the young birds peck at it, the parent regurgitates food for them to eat.

Great Black-backed Gull
ACTUAL SIZE IS 29 INCHES

ACTUAL SIZE

SHOREBIRDS

To entice a mate and advertise territory, a woodpecker strikes its beak against a hollow tree or dried branch and produces a rapid-fire, resonating drumming.

A green woodpecker relies on its short, rounded wings to fly the obstacle course of its dense forest home and to make controlled landings on tree trunks.

Woodpecker

With an insistent knock-knock-knocking, the great spotted woodpecker hammers directly into the workplace of wood-boring insects. A strong, sharp beak, acute hearing, shock-absorbing head bones, and massive neck muscles make possible this particular style of hunting.

Some homeowners wish their neighborhood woodpeckers could be seen but not heard. These inventive birds produce an enormous racket by drumming on metal roofing, stovepipes, and even satellite dishes.

A crucial milestone in the bonding of a downy woodpecker couple is their agreement on a nesting site. If the birds cannot settle on a single tree, the relationship quickly dissolves.

A woodpecker couple diligently excavates a nest cavity out of a dead tree stub or perhaps in a diseased, living tree. Nestlings later enjoy the sawdust cushion left over from construction.

Gregarious acorn woodpeckers hoard surplus food by wedging up to 50,000 nuts into holes made in a centrally located storage tree.

Song Birds

Mockingbird

Nightingale

"'Tis always morning somewhere, and above
The awakening continents, from shore to shore,
Somewhere the birds are singing ever more."
--HENRY WADSWORTH LONGFELLOW

Nightingale

Luscinia megarhynchos

It is too hard to equal its breath.
Hold the bird call in the left hand and
turn (with thumb and forefinger) the wooden part
using a light pressure. By rubbing one against the other
one can reproduce the Nightingale's song

© QUELLE EST BELLE COMPANY / L'ENFANT A LA FETE
product of france - modèle déposé

Eastern Meadowlark

Common Starling

Song Sparrow

Some birds just can't carry a tune. Vultures, for example, have few of the "music muscles" that control the scope of song. Songbirds, however, are the avian world's virtuosos. Genetically fine-tuned instruments for song. Twittering flutes, lilting violins, and lowing clarinets, songbirds perform in open-air arenas, free of charge.

But for the birds, the utterings serve basic functions of life -- as territorial markers, danger signals, mate enticers. Whether they enjoy their songs as much as humans do remains one of nature's secrets.

Song Birds

Red-eyed Vireo

Black-throated Green Warbler

Black-throated Blue Warbler

A BIRD IS RARELY FOOLED BY A HUMAN'S IMITATION OF ITS CALL. BIRD SONGS ARE SO COMPLEX THAT AN IMPERSONATOR RARELY EVEN COMES CLOSE. WITH SOME SONGS OF 80 NOTES PER SECOND AND UP TO 4 OVERLAPPING NOTES PRODUCED AT ONCE, IT WOULD TAKE THE ENTIRE MORMON TABERNACLE CHOIR TO GIVE A PROPER APPROXIMATION.

Western Tanager

Cape May Warbler

Song Sparrow

Song Birds

LOUD, PENETRATING SONG IS VITAL TO THE SONGBIRD'S SURVIVAL IN THE TANGLE OF BRANCHES AND LEAVES WHERE VISUAL DISPLAYS ARE LARGELY INEFFECTIVE.

The song calls attention to the pint-size performers and communicates that potential mates are welcome, intruders are not.

It seems a contradiction to call a bird-song afficionado a bird watcher. The most dynamic performers often vocalize behind a curtain of dense foliage, and only occasionally does the birder catch full sight of the virtuoso.

In some species, a hatchling is born knowing the basic score of its species' song, but only after hearing its elders sing over and over does the apprentice become a master.

The male vireo is a voracious eater and vociferous songster who, like a bizarre ventriloquist, sings even as he gobbles down insect after insect. Among those species that sing incessantly, the red-eyed vireo holds the avian record with over 22,000 performances in a single day.

Birds that sing from exposed perches sing short but sweet phrases, while birds in less vulnerable spots often sing for much longer periods of time. The grasshopper warbler, well hidden in the woodland thicket, performs a solo that lasts for more than 2 minutes.

Where songbirds choose to perform varies. The black-throated blue warbler consistently sings from limbs near the ground, a black-throated green warbler from midway up, and the cape may warbler calls out from the treetops.

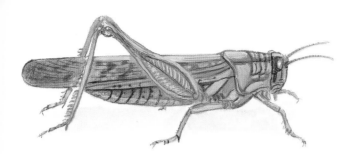

CRANES ARE VORACIOUS EATERS!

*I*T IS UNLIKELY THAT THE WHOOPING CRANE WILL EXPAND, UNAIDED, BEYOND ITS CURRENT WORLDWIDE POPULATION OF ABOUT 200 BIRDS. THIS CRANE RETURNS UNWAVERINGLY TO THE SAME TEXAS COAST REGION EVERY WINTER, A REFUGE OF LIMITED SIZE THAT ACCOMMODATES THE CURRENT NUMBER OF BIRDS BUT DOES NOT ALLOW FOR EXPANSION.

*U*NLIKE THE WHOOPING CRANE, THE SANDHILL CRANE IS AN ABUNDANT SPECIES THAT, THROUGH HUMAN ASSISTANCE, HELPS BOLSTER THE POPULATION OF ITS STRUGGLING RELATIVE. ORNITHOLOGISTS REMOVE 1 EGG FROM THE WHOOPING CRANE'S DOUBLE CLUTCH (THE BIRD LAYS 2 EGGS BUT USUALLY BRINGS ONLY 1 TO TERM) AND INTRODUCES IT INTO THE NEST OF A SANDHILL, WHICH BECOMES THE ENDANGERED BIRD'S SURROGATE PARENT.

Sandhill Crane - Actual size

Whooping Crane - Actual size

Crane

CAUGHT AND ATE 800 TEXAS GRASSHOPPERS

ONE INSATIABLE WHOOPING CRANE

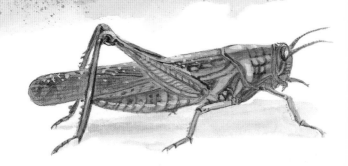

Cranes are among the avian world's most expressive dancers. Bobbing, bowing, swinging their nimble bodies, and, if the mood strikes, leaping into the air while loudly whooping, cranes perform a dramatic courtship ritual, which has been mimicked in the dances of African tribes, the Ainu of Japan, Australian Aborigines, and Native Americans.

Whooping Crane

ACTUAL SIZE IS: 50 INCHES

The tallest North American bird, the whooping crane stands almost 5 feet high, and its wingspan matches that of an eagle, at 8 feet.

IN A LITTLE OVER AN HOUR!

WHAT A HUMAN STRUGGLES TO ACCOMPLISH WITH A HAND-HELD NUTCRACKER, A PARROT HANDLES EASILY WITH ITS POWERFUL BEAK.

THOUGH THE HYACINTHINE MACAW IS A HIGHLY SOUGHT AFTER CAGE-BIRD, IT IS DEBATABLE WHETHER OR NOT IT MAKES A GOOD PET. CONFINED, THE BIRD LOUDLY ANNOUNCES ITS BOREDOM LIKE AN UNTRULY ALARM CLOCK, SCREECHING OR SQUAWKING AT ALL HOURS OF THE DAY. IF DENIED CONSTANT ATTENTION FROM ITS HUMAN "MATE," IT TURNS AS SULLEN AS A JEALOUS LOVER. AND THE MACAW'S POWERFUL BILL CAN EASILY SNIP THROUGH THE WIRE MESH OF MOST CAGES.

WHILE MANY CAGE-BIRDS HAVE CLIPPED WINGS TO INHIBIT FLIGHT, THE CURIOUS KAKAPO, OR OWL PARROT, OF NEW ZEALAND IS NATURALLY EARTHBOUND. THIS RARE AND HEAVILY BUILT PARROT HOPS AND GLIDES DOWN HILLSIDES ALONG WELL WORN PATHS TOWARD ITS FEEDING GROUNDS.

Sulphur-Crested Cockatoo

ACTUAL SIZE IS 18 INCHES

COCKATOOS ARE PLUMED IN WHITES, GRAYS, AND BLACKS, OFTEN WITH RED OR YELLOW PATCHES OF COLOR. ON SIGHTING A PREDATOR, A FLOCK OF SULPHUR-CRESTED COCKATOOS RISES IN A WHITE CLOUD AND, WITH CRESTS RAISED LIKE HACKLES, SHATTERS THE FOREST CALM WITH EAR-PIERCING SHRIEKS OF PROTEST.

THE PARROT FAMILY'S SIGNATURE BILL CATERS PERFECTLY TO THE BIRD'S DIET; THE HOOKED TIP SCRAPES OUT FRUIT PULP WHILE THE JAW AT THE BASE NEATLY CRACKS OPEN NUTRITIOUS SEEDS AND NUTS.

AS IF THEIR RAUCUS CALLS DID NOT DRAW ENOUGH ATTENTION, MANY PARROTS, INCLUDING THE SHIMMERY SCARLET MACAW AND THE GLOSSY BLUE-AND-YELLOW MACAW, PROFFER A DAZZLING DISPLAY OF COLOR.

SOME PARROT SPECIES ARE AMAZING MIMICS OF THE HUMAN VOICE. AFTER PATIENT TRAINING, PARROTS HAVE BEEN KNOWN TO CURSE LIKE A SAILOR, BARK LIKE A DOG, OR SING AS WELL, OR AS POORLY, AS ITS VOCAL COACH.

Blue-and-Yellow Macaw

ACTUAL SIZE IS 31 INCHES

Scarlet Macaw
ACTUAL SIZE IS 36 INCHES

Purple Gallinule
ACTUAL SIZE IS 12-14 INCHES

𝓐 GALLINULE'S WIDELY SPACED TOES ARE AS AGILE AS HUMAN FINGERS AND WORK LIKE SNOWSHOES, ALLOWING THE BIRD TO STRIDE ATOP LILY PADS, TO SKIP ACROSS WATER BEFORE TAKEOFF, AND TO WADE WITHOUT SINKING INTO SOFT MUD.

𝓣HE PURPLE GALLINULE IS DRESSED TO THE NINES IN THE SPECIES' MOST FLAMBOYANT FEATHER COLORS, YET THIS PAINFULLY SHY BIRD BARELY MAKES APPEARANCES OUTSIDE OF ITS MARSH HOME.

𝓑EWARE: A GALLINULE'S LOUD, ALARMING CACKLE MAY SCARE THE HIP BOOTS OFF A CURIOUS BIRDER TRESPASSING IN ITS SWAMPY TERRITORY.

GET TOO CLOSE AND THE COMMON GALLINULE RETORTS WITH ITS EAR-SHATTERING SQUEAL, KIK-KIK-KIK!

LEAST BITTERN
ACTUAL SIZE IS 11-14 INCHES

Sensing danger, a bittern will mimic a cattail stalk by pointing its beak straight up to the sky, stretching its body thin, bulging its low-set eyes forward, and even rocking with the furry plants in the breeze. If the disguise fails, the bird may cause a ruckus, puffing itself up and flapping its wings to appear more threatening.

The least bittern's plaited nest is a mass of vegetation anchored to living bulrushes and cattails. Above, a woven canopy provides shade and camouflage. Below, feeding platforms constructed of bent stalks allow for fishing in water that is too deep for wading.

Marsh Birds

"A Wise Old Owl Lived In An Oak;

Short-eared Owl
ACTUAL SIZE IS 13-17 INCHES

Dusky Horned Owl
ACTUAL SIZE IS 24 INCHES

American Hawk Owl
ACTUAL SIZE IS 14½-17½ INCHES

It IS TOUGH TO SNEAK UP ON AN OWL: ITS AMAZING HEARING AND ASTONISHING ABILITY TO ROTATE ITS HEAD NEARLY FULL CIRCLE MAKE IT AN EXCELLENT SENTRY.

Barn Owl
ACTUAL SIZE IS 17 INCHES

Great Gray Owl
ACTUAL SIZE IS 27 INCHES

Long-eared Owl
ACTUAL SIZE IS 14 INCHES

Flying SLOWLY, STEALTHILY, IN COMPLETE DARKNESS A FEW FEET ABOVE THE FOREST FLOOR, THE BARN OWL LISTENS FOR THE HIGH-PITCHED SQUEALS OF MICE AND OTHER SMALL ANIMALS, THEN, WITH TALONS EXTENDED, SUDDENLY SWOOPS DOWN UPON ITS VICTIM.

Like MANY OWLS, THE GREAT GRAY OWL RARELY BUILDS ITS OWN NEST; IT SIMPLY BORROWS ONE VACATED BY ANOTHER BIRD. TO MAKE ITS ADOPTED HOME ITS OWN BEFORE EGG-LAYING, THE OWL SPRUCES UP THE INTERIOR BY ADDING A FEW NEW FEATHERS, MOSS PIECES, OR TWIGS.

The Less He Spoke The More He Heard;

The More He Saw The Less He Spoke:

Snowy Owl
ACTUAL SIZE IS 24 INCHES

Resplendent in its coat of fluffy white feathers, the Snowy Owl is perfectly concealed in Arctic terrain.

Saw-whet Owl
ACTUAL SIZE IS 7 INCHES

One of the calls made by the Saw-whet Owl sounds dreadfully like its own name: a saw being repeatedly sharpened with a file.

Great Horned Owl
ACTUAL SIZE IS 21½ INCHES

The Great Horned Owl, a common resident of urban parks, is fairly tolerant of humans, unlike other owl species. But do not get too close to its nest! This protective bird will attack a curious human as if it were nothing more than a mouse or shrew.

Rocky Mountain Pygmy Owl
ACTUAL SIZE IS 6½ INCHES

OWL

Humans may recognize owls by their charming hoots, ear-splitting screeches, and inquisitive whoo-whoos, but owls are incomparably silent predators. Softly fringed flight feathers muffle the sound of flapping wings and silence the owl's deadly approach.

Why Can't We All Be Like That Bird?"
-- EDWARD HERSEY RICHARDS

INCE 1600, MORE THAN 100 BIRD SPECIES WORLDWIDE HAVE BECOME EXTINCT. IN NORTH AMERICA ALONE, ROUGHLY 75 SPECIES ARE CLASSIFIED AS "ENDANGERED" OR "THREATENED," LARGELY THE DIRECT RESULT OF HUMAN ACTIVITY. NO CONTINENT IS CURRENTLY WITHOUT BIRDS IN JEOPARDY.

WORLDWIDE, UP TO 3 MILLION WATERFOWL DIE ANNUALLY FROM LEAD POISONING, THE CONSEQUENCE OF WIDESPREAD HUNTING. IRONICALLY, EVEN HUNTERS WITH THE POOREST AIM CAN CAUSE HARM. LEAD PELLETS THAT MISS THEIR MARK FALL INTO THE BIRDS' FEEDING GROUNDS, AND A SINGLE, SWALLOWED PELLET CAN CAUSE DEATH.

THE MOST INSIDIOUS AND PERILOUS THREATS TO BIRDS HAVE COME IN THE NAME OF PROGRESS FOR HUMANITY. THE USE OF ORGANIC MERCURY PESTICIDES TO PROTECT RICE FIELDS, FOR EXAMPLE, COMPLETELY DESTROYED THE WHITE STORKS OF JAPAN. OFFSHORE DUMPING, DREDGING, AND SPILLAGE WREAK ROUTINE HAVOC ON COUNTLESS SHORELINES AND SHOREBIRDS. ALL OVER THE GLOBE, THE FILLING OF SWAMPLANDS, THE CUTTING OF FORESTS, AND THE DRAINING OF MARSHES DISTURB SPECIES THAT CANNOT ADJUST TO THE SUDDEN CHANGES. IN THE TROPICAL RAIN FORESTS, SOME SPECIES OF BIRDS MAY BECOME EXTINCT BEFORE THEY ARE EVEN DISCOVERED.

to sing when their groves are cut down?"
— HENRY DAVID THOREAU

As humans, it may be difficult to relate to a species like the red-cockaded woodpecker, whose very existence depends on a particular nesting site.

The typical practice of removing dead trees from a forest inevitably "removes" most woodpecker species as well. In South Carolina, in the last isolated patches of old forest, there are probably more warning signs on trees identifying the endangered red-cockaded woodpecker than there are actual birds.

Over time, birds such as this have carved out specific niches in nature that have made them extremely vulnerable to changes in the environment. Sadly, humans often overlook their needs and evolution simply does not happen fast enough to help them adapt and survive.

A half-mile stretch of 2,000 greater flamingos stand like lawn ornaments, casting powdery-pink reflections into the calm water as they perform their one-footed balancing act, made possible by a strong, rigid body frame and a low center of gravity.

FLAMINGO BRAND GROWN IN USA
BROGDEXED
PINELLAS COUNTY
GRAPEFRUIT - ORANGE
F. L. SKINNER
DUNEDIN FLORIDA

A flamingo's pink and red plumage is the colorful result of the adage: you are what you eat. The bird extracts a natural dye from shrimp and algae that tints its feathers.

FLAMINGO

FLAMINGOS FEED BY POKING THEIR HEADS UPSIDE DOWN INTO SHALLOW WATER AND TRAWLING WITH THEIR SIEVE LIKE BILLS. THE UPPER BILL ACTS LIKE A LID; THE LOWER RESEMBLES A TROUGH. A MOUTHFUL OF WATER IS FILTERED OUT, LEAVING BEHIND THE NUTRITIOUS CATCH.

Hooded Merganser

Canvasback

Common Goldeneye

Bufflehead

Duck

Wood Duck

Blue-winged Teal

Cinnamon Teal

Wigeon

DESPITE VAST DIVERSITY, THE 147 DUCK SPECIES CAN BE DIVIDED INTO 2 SIMPLE CATAGORIES: "DIVERS," WHICH PLUNGE COMPLETELY UNDERWATER FOR FOOD, AND "DABBLERS," WHICH SKIM FOOD FROM THE WATER'S SURFACE OR TIP FORWARD, TAIL POINTED TO THE SKY, TO FEED IN THE SHALLOWS.

GRUNTS, HOOTS, HONKS, AND COOS COMPOSE THE MALE DUCK'S EXTENSIVE REPERTOIRE, BUT THE SIGNATURE QUACK COMES ONLY FROM THE FEMALE.

WOOD DUCKS PREFER TO NEST IN HOLLOW BRANCHES, ABANDONED WOODPECKER HOLES, AND NATURAL TREE-TRUNK CAVITIES IF SUCH HOLES ARE AVAILABLE. ALL TOO COMMONLY, THOUGH, HUMANS DEMOLISH THE BIRDS' NATURAL HOMES WITH THEIR PRUNING SHEARS AND CHAIN SAWS.

ONCE A YEAR, MALE DUCKS RAPIDLY SHED THEIR BREEDING PLUMAGE, LITTERING THE GROUND WITH WHAT RESEMBLES THE AFTERMATH OF AN ALL-OUT PILLOW FIGHT. UNTIL NEW FEATHERS GROW IN, THE BIRDS ARE GROUNDED FOR A MONTH OR MORE.

Spur-wing Goose

Bar-headed Goose

Cape Barren Goose

Barnacle Goose

Goose

Canada Goose

When nest-building, ducks and geese generally make do with whatever lies at their webbed feet. They drag dead leaves, weeds, and mosses, or pass them over the shoulder, to form a pile at the chosen ground site.

Canada geese mate for life and remain equally faithful to the same nesting site year after year after year.

Something amazing happens when a gathering of geese takes flight in formation: it changes from a "gaggle" to a "skein."

Ross' Goose

White-fronted Goose

Emperor Goose

"Then, upon the velvet sinking, I betook myself to linking
    fancy unto fancy, thinking what this ominous bird of
Yore--
    What this grim, ungainly, ghastly, gaunt, and ominous
Bird of yore
    Meant in croaking 'Nevermore!'"

-- Edgar Allan Poe, "The Raven"

OMINOUS

*F*OLKLORE HAS CONSISTENTLY CAST BLACK-PLUMED BIRDS AS FOREBODING OR EVIL. ONE GREEK LEGEND RECOUNTS THE PURE WHITE RAVEN THAT STOLE WATER, ONLY TO BE PUNISHED BY THE GODS BY HAVING ITS FEATHERS BLACKENED. IN ANOTHER LEGEND, 2 CROWS, HORRIBLE TATTLERS, CROAKED MESSAGES OF THE MISDEEDS OF HUMANS TO ODIN, RULER OF THE NORSE GODS.

CROW ACTUAL SIZE

BIRDS

*H*IGH OVERHEAD, SEVERAL LARGE TURKEY VULTURES, WITH UPTILTED, MOTIONLESS WINGS, CIRCLE OMINOUSLY, AWAITING THE DEMISE OF THEIR VICTIM FAR BELOW. ONCE DEATH COMES, THE VULTURES DESCEND IN A RUSH. THE BIRDS MAKE QUICK WORK OF THE CARRION SMORGASBORD, ABLE TO PICK CLEAN THE BONES OF AN ANTELOPE, FOR EXAMPLE, IN UNDER 20 MINUTES.

A VULTURE DOES NOT SING; INSTEAD, IT MAKES RUDIMENTARY GRUNTS AND HISSES TO GET ITS POINT ACROSS.

*T*HE UNCONTESTED "BRAINS" OF THE BIRD WORLD, MEMBERS OF THE CROW FAMILY ARE EXTREMELY CUNNING AND BOLD. A THIEVING HOODED CROW WAS ONCE OBSERVED PULLING UP FISH CAUGHT ON AN ICE FISHERMAN'S UNATTENDED LINE.

A RAVEN WILL EAT PRACTICALLY ANYTHING THAT DOES NOT PUT UP A FIGHT.

Raven
ACTUAL SIZE
IS 26 INCHES

Turkey
Vulture
ACTUAL SIZE IS 32 INCHES

THE CORMORANT IS SHROUDED NOT ONLY IN DARK, DUSKY FEATHERS, BUT IN HUMAN BIAS AS WELL. DEEMED "UNCLEAN" IN DEUTERONOMY AND SYNONYMOUS WITH "GLUTTONY" BY CHAUCER, THE CORMORANT HAS ALSO BEEN DEFAMED BY MILTON AND SHAKESPEARE WITH THEIR ALLUSIONS TO SATAN AND THE "DEVOURER OF LIFE."

DIVING FROM THE SURFACE, A CORMORANT MAY REMAIN UNDERWATER FOR UP TO A MINUTE, DEFTLY TAILGATING A FISH WITH POWERFUL THRUSTS OF ITS LARGE WEBBED FEET. THE BIRD REGAINS THE SURFACE WITH THE FISH SNAGGED CROSSWISE IN ITS SLENDER HOOKED BEAK, TOSSES THE CATCH INTO THE AIR, AND SWALLOWS IT HEAD FIRST.

THE WORD CORMORANT MEANS "CROW OF THE SEA," BUT THIS BIG BLACK WATERBIRD IS CLOSELY RELATED TO THE PELICAN FAMILY.

THE DOUBLE-CRESTED CORMORANT PERCHES ON A BUOY OR A SUN-TOASTED ROCK AND DRIES ITS FEATHERS IN A SPREAD-WINGED DRACULA POSE.

Crow
ACTUAL SIZE
IS
21 INCHES

Double-crested
Cormorant
ACTUAL SIZE IS
32 INCHES

MIGRATION

IS FREQUENTLY A DANGEROUS, EXHAUSTING, AND FATAL ORDEAL. AND YET THE IMPULSE TO MIGRATE IS SO DEEPLY INGRAINED THAT EVEN SOME BIRDS IN CAGES-- WELL-FED AND CARED FOR--EXPERIENCE "MIGRATORY FEVER" AT THE TIME OF YEAR WHEN THEIR FREE RELATIVES NORMALLY TAKE WING.

BIRDS THAT MIGRATE ARE BORN WITH A WANDERLUST THAT IS LINKED INDELIBLY TO THEIR INSTINCT FOR SURVIVAL. SCIENCE CONTENDS THAT THESE BIRDS POSSESS A POWERFUL "INNER COMPASS," AN INHERITED ABILITY TO NAVIGATE, USING THE SUN AND STARS, THAT UNERRINGLY POINTS THEM IN THE RIGHT DIRECTION. OTHER STUDIES SUGGEST THAT THE EARTH'S MAGNETIC FIELD, TOPOGRAPHICAL LANDMARKS, ODORS, AND EVEN LOW-FREQUENCY SOUND WAVES MIGHT PLAY A ROLE.

THIS SENSE IS SO ACCURATE THAT ANCIENT NAVIGATORS SOMETIMES TURNED TO MIGRATING BIRDS TO HELP KEEP THEM ON COURSE. IN FACT, IN 1492 THE CREW OF THE SPANISH SHIP PINTA SIGHTED A MASS OF BIRDS FLYING SOUTH. FOLLOWING THEIR LEAD, CHRISTOPHER COLUMBUS DISCOVERED THE NEW WORLD.

Not all birds migrate, however, and some make short, though arduous trips.

QUITE FRANKLY, NO ONE KNOWS JUST HOW IT WORKS; ONE EXPLANATION CANNOT BE APPLIED TO ALL SPECIES.

WHAT URGES AN ARCTIC TERN TO LEAVE ITS NORTH POLE BREEDING GROUNDS EACH YEAR AND FLY 10,000 MILES ACROSS THE GLOBE TO THE SOUTHERN POLAR REGIONS, AND THEN, AFTER A SEASON, TO MAKE THE LENGTHY RETURN TRIP?

THE LIKELY ANSWER TO THIS PUZZLE, STRANGELY ENOUGH, LIES IN THE FINAL DAYS OF THE ICE AGE.

AS GLACIERS SLOWLY RETREATED, FRESH LANDS AND FOOD SOURCES WERE REVEALED. ENTICED BY THE RICH SUMMER VEGETATION, BIRDS WERE DRAWN FARTHER AND FARTHER NORTH. YET, AS THE SEASON WANED, THEY WERE FORCED TO FLY SOUTH AGAIN TO ESCAPE THE COLDER TEMPERATURES AND TO SEARCH FOR NEW SOURCES OF FOOD.

IT IS BELIEVED THAT THIS PATTERN, REPEATED OVER THE CENTURIES, EVOLVED INTO THE INSTINCT TO MIGRATE.

The Emperor Penguin does not build or burrow or sculpt a nest in the barren Antarctic terrain. Instead, the single, large egg is placed right at the male bird's feet, where it is cradled snugly beneath a patch on his belly which is specially adapted to keep the egg warm.

Thousands of duty-bound male Emperors huddle together for extra warmth, frozen in place for the grueling 2-month incubation of the egg. During this time, females are on leave from family obligations, but return just before the hatching to relieve the males, seriously weakened from their nesting ordeal.

Penguins are not able to fly, but then, they do not need to. These well-insulated birds feed exclusively at sea, where they swim and dive hundreds of feet in icy waters using their small wings as oars and their webbed feet as powerful prorellers.

Emperor Penguin Actual size is 48 inches

PENGUIN

ENGUINS ARE NATIVE TO THE SOUTHERN HEMISPHERE, YET NOT ALL ARE AT HOME IN THE SNOW AND ICE OF THE SOUTH POLE. THE GALAPAGOS PENGUIN AND OTHER SPECIES PREFER THE SUN AND SAND OF THE TROPICS.

WITH FEET SET WELL BACK ON ITS BODY, THE AWKWARD PENGUIN WOBBLES ON LAND LIKE AN ANIMATED BOWLING PIN, AND OFTEN TOPPLES ONTO ITS STOMACH TO TOBOGGAN DOWN ICY SLOPES.

TO THE HUMAN EYE, A COLONY OF SEVERAL MILLION PENGUINS MAY APPEAR IDENTICALLY DRESSED IN THE SAME DAPPER TUXEDO, BUT DISTINCTIVE BODY MARKINGS AND RALLYING CALLS ENABLE INDIVIDUAL BIRDS TO LOCATE LOST YOUNG OR MATES WITH UNFAILING ACCURACY.

Galapagos Penguin
ACTUAL SIZE IS 20 INCHES

European

The European cuckoo's namesake call is heard in works by Beethoven, Haydn, and Vivaldi, and announces the hour from "cuckoo clocks" around the world.

Cuckoo

Even though the cuckoo's name is also an adjective meaning "addle brained," the European species clearly defies such definition with its remarkable ability to deceive. To hatch its young, the calculating bird selects the nest of a suitable foster parent, which it momentarily frightens away with its somewhat hawklike appearance, before laying an egg whose color and size closely matches those found within. It may even remove 1 of the original eggs to avoid suspicion of the imposter.

Rivalry between the foster baby and its nest-mates is ruthless. The young cuckoo often hatches first and instinctively ejects from the nest all eggs or helpless newborns it encounters. As an "only child," the bird has the best chance for survival.

At 3 weeks of age, the cuckoo hatchling weighs 50 times more than it did at birth. One of nature's most absurd tragicomedies unfolds as the diminutive adoptive parent -- a reed warbler or meadow pipit, for example -- feverishly collects food to satisfy a nestling more than twice its size!

CHOOSE AN ELEGANT ADJECTIVE AND IT HAS PROBABLY BEEN USED TO DESCRIBE THE SWAN.

THE HEAVY-BODIED, LONG-NECKED, SMOOTH-GLIDING SWAN IS THE PICTURESQUE MONARCH OF LAKES AND SLOW-MOVING RIVERS. THE TRUMPETER SWAN IS THE LARGEST WATERFOWL IN NORTH AMERICA WITH OUTER WING FEATHERS UP TO 18 INCHES LONG AND A TOTAL BODY WEIGHT OF ALMOST 28 POUNDS.

ALL SWANS HAVE GLORIOUS, RINGING VOICES WHICH ARE REFLECTED IN SOME OF THE NAMES IN THIS SPECIES: THE TRUMPETER SWAN, THE WHISTLING SWAN, THE WHOOPER SWAN. EVEN THE NORMALLY SOFT-SPOKEN MUTE SWAN HONKS LOUDLY WHEN DISTURBED, AND ITS WHINING WHEE-YOU IS A COMMON SOUND ON PARK PONDS.

Swan

SWAN SONG (N.) 1: A SONG OF GREAT SWEETNESS SAID TO BE SUNG BY A DYING SWAN. 2: A FAREWELL APPEARANCE OR FINAL ACT OR PRONOUNCEMENT.

"SWAN" FOUNTPENS

The Pens with the Smoothest Gold Nibs

In a Greek myth, Zeus took the form of a majestic swan to approach the beautiful Queen Leda as she bathed. Nine months later, Leda laid an enormous egg that contained Helen of Troy and the twins, who later became the constellation Gemini.

Whistling Swan
ACTUAL SIZE

A young swan, called a cygnet, is the ugly duckling of fairy tales, with dull gray feathers that last for about 3 years.

"Leda and the Swan,"
School of Leonardo.

HERONS ARE MASTER STALKERS OF FISH. THEY STAND IN THE SHALLOWS, MOVING VERY LITTLE AND VERY STEALTHILY, WAITING FOR A FISH TO SWIM WITHIN THEIR GRASP.

MANY FISH-EATING BIRDS, LIKE HERONS AND STORKS, HAVE WHITE UNDERSIDES, A HELPFUL AID IN FISH-CATCHING: THEIR PREY CANNOT SEE WHITE AGAINST THE SKY AS EASILY AS THEY CAN DARKER COLORS.

STORK & HERON

Great Blue Heron
ACTUAL SIZE IS 52 INCHES

THESE ABLE-BODIED FLYERS HAVE A SPECIAL PLACE IN ANCIENT FOLKLORE. AGES AGO, HUMANS BELIEVED THAT SMALL, WEAK BIRDS HITCHHIKED ACROSS THE MEDITERRANEAN ON A STORK'S BACK. AT THE SAME TIME, STORKS WERE ALWAYS SIGHTED OVER THE HOUSE WHERE A BABY HAD BEEN BORN, AND FROM THIS GREW THE BELIEF THAT IT WAS THE STORK THAT DELIVERED BABIES. EVEN TODAY, STORKS ARE RECOGNIZED INTERNATIONALLY AS A SYMBOL OF BIRTH.

THE AMERICAN WOOD STORK WORKS ITS WAY THROUGH MUDDY WATER FEELING FOR ITS FOOD, SWEEPING ITS BILL LEFT AND RIGHT LIKE A BEACHCOMBER'S METAL DETECTOR. WHEN THIS EXTREMELY SENSITIVE TOOL FINDS A TREASURE -- A FISH, FROG, OR SNAKE -- IT SNAPS SHUT WITH THE FORCE AND SPEED OF A STEEL TRAP.

American Wood Stork
ACTUAL SIZE IS 47 INCHES

DELIVERY

French

French

French

Danish

English

Birds, eggs, feathers, and nests are best treasured from afar.

Bird buttons are another thing altogether ...

Japanese

Scattered across these pages is an international collection of bird buttons. Some have fastened the breeches of 17th century German folk and others have adorned children of Victorian England enchanted with storybook characters. Still others celebrate the French Art Nouveau stained glass enameling technique called Plique-à-jour, symbolize longevity with a thousand cranes on Chinese and Japanese vestments, and were mass produced in the American Bakelite plastic of the 1930s.

French

American

American

German

English

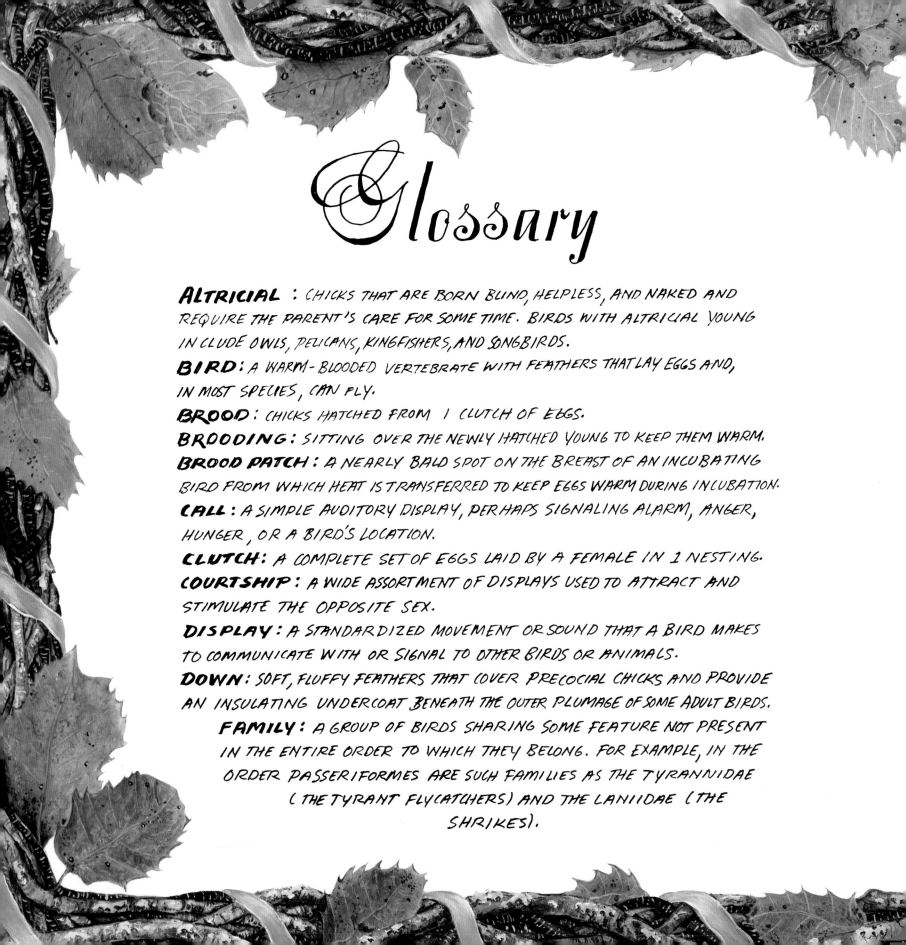

Glossary

ALTRICIAL : CHICKS THAT ARE BORN BLIND, HELPLESS, AND NAKED AND REQUIRE THE PARENT'S CARE FOR SOME TIME. BIRDS WITH ALTRICIAL YOUNG INCLUDE OWLS, PELICANS, KINGFISHERS, AND SONGBIRDS.

BIRD: A WARM-BLOODED VERTEBRATE WITH FEATHERS THAT LAY EGGS AND, IN MOST SPECIES, CAN FLY.

BROOD: CHICKS HATCHED FROM 1 CLUTCH OF EGGS.

BROODING: SITTING OVER THE NEWLY HATCHED YOUNG TO KEEP THEM WARM.

BROOD PATCH : A NEARLY BALD SPOT ON THE BREAST OF AN INCUBATING BIRD FROM WHICH HEAT IS TRANSFERRED TO KEEP EGGS WARM DURING INCUBATION.

CALL : A SIMPLE AUDITORY DISPLAY, PERHAPS SIGNALING ALARM, ANGER, HUNGER, OR A BIRD'S LOCATION.

CLUTCH: A COMPLETE SET OF EGGS LAID BY A FEMALE IN 1 NESTING.

COURTSHIP : A WIDE ASSORTMENT OF DISPLAYS USED TO ATTRACT AND STIMULATE THE OPPOSITE SEX.

DISPLAY: A STANDARDIZED MOVEMENT OR SOUND THAT A BIRD MAKES TO COMMUNICATE WITH OR SIGNAL TO OTHER BIRDS OR ANIMALS.

DOWN: SOFT, FLUFFY FEATHERS THAT COVER PRECOCIAL CHICKS AND PROVIDE AN INSULATING UNDERCOAT BENEATH THE OUTER PLUMAGE OF SOME ADULT BIRDS.

FAMILY: A GROUP OF BIRDS SHARING SOME FEATURE NOT PRESENT IN THE ENTIRE ORDER TO WHICH THEY BELONG. FOR EXAMPLE, IN THE ORDER PASSERIFORMES ARE SUCH FAMILIES AS THE TYRANNIDAE (THE TYRANT FLYCATCHERS) AND THE LANIIDAE (THE SHRIKES).

FLEDGLING: A CHICK THAT HAS LEFT THE NEST BUT IS STILL DEPENDENT ON ITS PARENTS FOR SOME OR ALL OF ITS FOOD.

HATCHLING: A CHICK THAT HAS JUST EMERGED FROM ITS EGG.

INCUBATION: PERIOD WHEN EITHER PARENT COVERS THE CLUTCH WITH ITS BODY IN ORDER TO REGULATE THE EGGS' TEMPERATURE AND TO FURTHER THEIR DEVELOPMENT.

MIGRATION: MASS MOVEMENT OF BIRDS BETWEEN 2 WIDELY SEPARATED AREAS, GENERALLY BETWEEN BREEDING AND NONBREEDING GROUNDS.

MOLT: TO SHED THE OUTER PLUMAGE AND REPLACE IT WITH NEW FEATHERS; USUALLY OCCURS AFTER BREEDING SEASON.

NESTLING: A HATCHED BIRD THAT REMAINS IN THE NEST AND IS CARED FOR BY THE PARENTS OR OTHER ADULTS.

ORDER: A LARGE GROUP OF BIRDS SHARING CERTAIN INTERNAL CHARACTERISTICS. FOR EXAMPLE, PERCHING BIRDS FORM THE ORDER PASSERIFORMES, AND PIGEONS AND DOVES FORM THE ORDER COLUMBIFORMES.

PRECOCIAL: CHICKS THAT ARE BORN COVERED WITH DOWN, WITH EYES WIDE OPEN, AND WITH THE ABILITY TO RUN ABOUT ALMOST IMMEDIATELY. BIRDS WITH PRECOCIAL YOUNG INCLUDE DOMESTIC CHICKENS, DUCKS, PLOVERS, AND SHOREBIRDS.

PREEN: USING THE BEAK LIKE A COMB TO SMOOTH AND TRIM FEATHERS.

SONG: A COMPLEX AUDITORY DISPLAY THAT MAY BE PARTIALLY INHERITED AND PARTIALLY LEARNED; LOUDEST AND MOST FREQUENT DURING BREEDING SEASON.

SPECIES: A CLASSIFICATION FOR BIRDS WITHIN AN ORDER THAT LOOK ALIKE, ACT ALIKE, AND INTERBREED. FOR EXAMPLE, THE YELLOW-RUMPED WARBLER IS A SPECIES IN THE FAMILY EMBERIZIDAE OF THE ORDER PASSERIFORMES.

TERRITORY: ANY AREA THAT A BIRD DEFENDS AGAINST OTHERS.

More About Birds, Eggs, Feathers, and Nests

IN THE UNITED KINGDOM:

BRITISH TRUST FOR CONSERVATION VOLUNTEERS, 36 ST. MARY'S STREET, WALLINGFORD OX1 0EU

COUNCIL FOR ENVIRONMENTAL CONSERVATION, ZOOLOGICAL GARDENS, REGENTS PARK, LONDON NW1 4RY

WATCH, C/O ROYAL SOCIETY FOR NATURE CONSERVATION, 22 THE GREEN, NETTLEHAM, LINCOLN LN2 2NR

YOUNG ORNITHOLOGISTS' CLUB, THE LODGE, SANDY, BEDFORDSHIRE SG19 2DL

IN THE UNITED STATES:

THE CROW'S NEST, CORNELL LABORATORY OF ORNITHOLOGY, 159 SAPSUCKER WOODS ROAD, ITHACA, NY 14850

NATIONAL AUDUBON SOCIETY, 700 BROADWAY, NEW YORK, NY 10003

NATIONAL WILDLIFE FEDERATION, 1412 16TH STREET NW, WASHINGTON, D.C. 20036

SIERRA CLUB, 530 BUSH STREET, SAN FRANCISCO, CA 94108

WESTERN FOUNDATION OF VERTEBRATE ZOOLOGY, 439 CALLE SAN PABLO, CAMARILLO, CA 93010

IN AUSTRALIA AND CANADA:

ASSOCIATION OF SOUTH EAST FIELD NATURALISTS' SOCIETIES, P.O. BOX 1369, MOUNT GAMBIA, SOUTH AUSTRALIA 5290

CANADIAN NATURE FEDERATION, SUITE 203, 75 ALBERT STREET, OTTAWA K1P 6G1, CANADA

GOULD LEAGUE, C/O PUBLIC SCHOOL, MARY STREET, BEECROFT, NEW SOUTH WALES, 2119, AUSTRALIA

VICTORIAN FIELD NATURALISTS' CLUBS ASSOCIATIONS, C/O NATURAL HERBARIUM, SOUTH YARRO VICTORIA 3141, AUSTRALIA

"Une hirondelle ne fait pas le printemps.

ONE SWALLOW DOES NOT MAKE A SPRING."
CERVANTES, Don Quixote

I EXTEND HEARTFELT
GRATITUDE TO MANY
FOR ENRICHING THE
VISION OF THIS BOOK.

TO MY CREATIVE PARTNER
AND FRIEND, KRISTIN JOYCE,
AND TO HER EXUBERANT
HUSBAND, DON GUY.

TO OUR TALENTED
RESEARCHERS AND CONTRIBUTING
WRITERS, BILL HAYES AND STEVEN BYRNE.

TO OUR (TRULY!) ORIGINAL PUBLISHER, ANDY STEWART,
FOR HIS GENTLE GOOD NATURE, SMART ADVICE, AND UNSHAKABLE
CONFIDENCE IN THIS PROJECT. AND TO HIS GIFTED EXECUTIVE EDITOR, LESLIE STOKER AND ASSOCIATE,
ANDREA DANESE, FOR THEIR BRIGHT IDEAS AND KEEN ABILITY TO FINE-TUNE TEXT AND ART.

TO LLOYD KIFF AND HIS COLLEAGUE, MANUEL MARIN, FOR THEIR EXPERTISE AND FOR SHARING THE IMMENSE
AND OUTRAGEOUS COLLECTION OF NESTS AND EGGS AT THE WESTERN FOUNDATION OF VERTEBRATE
ZOOLOGY IN CAMARILLO, CALIFORNIA.

TO DIANA EPSTEIN AND MILLICENT SAFRO FOR THEIR FASCINATING KNOWLEDGE AND WORLD-CLASS BUTTON
COLLECTION AT TENDER BUTTONS IN NEW YORK.

TO OUR EXCITING, NEW HOME WITH SMITHMARK PUBLISHERS AND TO THE CONTAGIOUS ENTHUSIASM OF OUR
NEW PUBLISHER, MARTA HALLETT AND HER WONDERFUL EXECUTIVE EDITOR, ELIZABETH SULLIVAN.

TO OUR FRIENDS AND FAMILY WHO CONTINUE TO SHARE OUR JOY IN WATCHING THIS BOOK
SOAR TO BESTSELLING HEIGHTS!

Printed in Hong Kong by
Hong Kong Graphic and Printing Ltd.